HENRY CRABB ROBINSON

ON

BOOKS AND THEIR WRITERS

Date Due

HENRY CRABB ROBINSON IN 1860

From a sketch by G. Scharf

HENRY CRABB ROBINSON

ON

BOOKS AND THEIR WRITERS

EDITED BY

EDITH J. MORLEY

VOLUME THREE

LONDON

J. M. DENT AND SONS LIMITED

APPENDICES

APPENDIX I

Haddington, 29th April 1825.

(1) My dear Sir,—Knowing by repeated experience [2] your readiness to oblige, I make no scruple of applying to you in the present emergency, more especially as it relates to a department of business in which you take a deep interest for its own sake.

I have been engaged with an Edinburgh Bookseller to prepare three or perhaps four volumes of Translations from the German intended as specimens of their chief novel writers, with Prefaces, Lives, and Criticisms, and all the addenda which may serve to procure them a good-natured reception from the English public. My acquaintance with this branch of German literature is small, for it does not stand by any means in the highest favour with me, yet I calculate pretty confidently on being able to select a handful of sound wheat from the loads of chaff which I have yet examined only on the surface; and being naturally anxious to effect this as perfectly as possible, I have determined on soliciting the benefit of your knowledge and taste to aid me in my choice. The Bookseller leaves me unlimited freedom; he has no information on the subject, and few counsellors by whose light it were safe to walk. So far as I can judge his chief dependence seems to be on the *Volksmärchen* and *Rittererzählungen* of our neighbours; on Musäus, La Motte Fouqué, Lafontaine, and the other 'mob of gentlemen' who wrote for the venerable *Plebs* of the reading community. I dislike these people, but must not altogether neglect them. For the sake of popularity independent of merit, I must try to get a specimen or two from each of these notable person-ages; but my chief dependence is placed on Tieck, Richter, Wieland, and Goethe. From the last I have already determined to take *Werter, Melusine,* and what you told me Schlegel called

---

[1] Carlyle's letters are printed exactly as he wrote them, his capitals, spelling, abbreviations etc., being retained.
[2] There had not been much time. Crabb Robinson first made Carlyle's acquaintance on June 22nd 1824.

the *Mährchen aller Mährchen*.[1] In Wieland, I think, I shall find
an article or two in the *Hexameron von Rosenhain* or elsewhere,
valuable more for its author's than its own qualities, but giving
room for some discussion on *that* topic and therefore useful for
me. Of Richter I yet know little; I have looked into his *Herbst-
buminen* [*sic*], his *Flegeljahre*, and am now reading his *Fibel*. It is
easy to see already that next to Goethe (and Tieck?) he is the
best man in Germany; but his extravagance and barbarism will
render the task of selecting from him one of some difficulty.
The *Phantasien* which you lent me are all I know of Tieck; but I
must if possible have him included in my list, and some of his
smaller tales I hope will give me the opportunity. There is also
one Hoffmann whose *Elixiere des Teufels* was translated last year
in Edinburgh (with small success) concerning whom I could like
to have some further information. As to Claurens [*sic*], with his
Scherz und Ernst, I have got the book beside me, but put no faith
in it.

Now, my dear sir, could you of your own knowledge, or by
consulting with any of your German friends, afford me advice in
this matter? Could you learn for me which is Lafontaine's *best*
novel in one moderate volume? I have read his *Raphael* (in
French), his *Rudolph von Werdenberg*, and his *Tinchen* (in
German): there is genius in all of these; but whether any of them
is among the best of his half-a-century of works, I have no means
of ascertaining. Do you know the character of his *Sagen aus dem
Alterthüme* and his *Kleine Romane*? What is Tieck's best novel?
La Motte Fouqué's best novel or novels of the small sort? Is it
Ondine [*sic*]? This they wish me to translate, thinking it badly
done at present, but after reading the original, I despise it a good
deal. Can you tell me which is the Baroness La Motte Fouqué's
best? None of her little Tales are good: I must give a specimen
both of her and her husband, but I wish to make them very short,
for they are intrinsically very slender people.

In Edinburgh are several handsome collections of German
books, to most or all of which I have obtained or shall obtain
access, particularly to that in the Advocates' Library, one of the
most numerous if not the best selected in the Kingdom. Still
the quantity of books I shall have access to, compared with the
quantity I should wish to read before making a final choice is
inconsiderable; and as buying on the great scale is out of the
question, I am anxious to have the range of my examination

---

[1] 'In what book or treatise does he so call it?' [Carlyle translated
it in 1832.]

narrowed before commencing. For this purpose I put no small trust in you. I doubt not you will give me minutely your own thoughts on the matter; and transmit me those of your German friends in whose judgment you most rely. Has not Mrs. Aders (the lady who lent me *Wilhelm Meister*) great skill in such things? So great is my confidence in your goodness that if you could readily procure me a *loan* of any quantity of books likely to be of use to me, I should not hesitate to ask you to take the trouble of sending them for my perusal and criticism: consigned to a Bookseller in London, they might with the greatest ease and speed be sent to my Bookseller in Edinburgh, and thence to my abode. This seems a strange proposal, but when I look at your Don Quixote and Quevedo, I hardly think it stranger than your kindness of disposition. At all events, I count on your favouring me with your advice, the first hour you have leisure. I make no apologies for the trouble I am giving you, but I hope I shall not feel the obligation the less on that account. If you write within a week after this arrives (which would be very desirable), please to direct to No. 18 Salisbury Street, Edingh; if not till after that, it will be safer to say: Mainhill, Ecclefechan, Dumfries-shire, where I am to be all summer.

In a short while I mean to send you one of those *Schillers* that you may send it to Goethe: then I shall try to write less drily. At present I must stick to the naked point of business, and even this I can hardly yet handle in intelligible terms: crowds of people are about me. I must pray you to make the best of it, and to believe me always, with true esteem,

My dear sir,

Most faithfully yours,

THOMAS CARLYLE.

[Endorsed in Crabb Robinson's writing:]

La Motte Fouqué (Baroness) and Claurens [*sic*]—reprobated.
Wieland,[1] La Fontaine,[1] Familie von Halden [1] the best.
First collect[io]n of Moralische Erzählungen, Dankbarkeiten u. Liebe.
Messner, Der Hund des Melei. Tieck new ones lately trans-l[ate]d.
Richter, fragments from Titan. Reise des Feldpredigers Schmelzler a small work with (beautiful) notes. Neu-jahrsnacht.

[1] These also are 'reprobated,' i.e. omitted, from *German Romance*.

Klinger, Friederich Kind, small novelist.
Caroline Pickler.
La Motte. Der Zauber Ring. One volume. By far the best.
Franz Horn. Der ewige Jude. In an Almanach.
Hoffman.[1]—Serapions Brüder: in that Fräulein v. Scuderei u.
Phantasiespielen in wch.
Der goldene Topf.
A Miss Nancy Mitchell.
Amatonda.
Volksmärchen v. Musaeus.

Hoddam Hill, Dumfries-shire, 25th April, 1826.

(2) My dear Sir,—It is long since I ought to have thanked you
for your friendly and prompt answer to my last inquiries: and I do
so now with no very good grace, when I have a new favour to ask
of you. The Book of *German Novelists,* concerning which I took
your advice last spring, is actually in the Press: after much
loitering, groping, consulting, and passive and active meditating,
I at last fixed upon my men, began printing last January, and am
in hopes of being rid of the affair, if you can help me out of this
strait in which I am for the present entangled.

I am to have four volumes; *two* names in each of the first three;
and Goethe's *Wilhelm Meisters Wanderjahre* is to occupy the
fourth. Of these, the first and the *last* and half of the second are
already printed. Musäus, Fouqué, Tieck: Goethe with lives and
so forth; Hoffmann, Jean Paul, and Maler Müller [2] are still
desiderated. And like to be so, unless you can lend me a hand;
for the original works are not to be had in any *shop* of this Island;
and though I have sent for them both to Leipzig and Hamburg,
and the *invoice* from Fleischer in the former of these book-marts
reached me about a month ago, no glimpse of the ware itself
has yet come to light, not even a probability when it is to be
looked for. You will conceive the *nodus* of the case when I tell
you that in ten days unless some *Deus intersit,* Ballantyne with all
his Devils will be at a stand.

Of Hoffmann, I have a piece besides me that would answer, one
of his *Fantasiestücke in Callots Manier*; but I want much to see
his *Leben und Nachlass,* or any even the slenderest account of his
life; being ignorant at present even of the date of its termination.

[1] 'It has been far the worst and the most troublesome of them all.'
Letter to John Carlyle, May 1826. *Early Letters,* Norton, 1887.
[2] His works remained unobtainable and were not included among
Carlyle's translations.

With Jean Paul, also, I could contrive at a dead lift to 'help myself through'; on the faith of your recommendation I sent for *Schmelzle's Reise* and also for the *Leben Q[uintus] Fixlein*, with a Biography of the Illustrious Dead himself; the former works I suppose are on the road at present, but as for Biographies, Fleischer declares that though two *höchst interessante* Lives of Jean Paul are in the Press, no life whatever of him has yet come out of it. Nevertheless I have got the *Picnic und Dejeuner dansant zu Kuhschnappel* of Richter here, and if no better might be, with this I could serve my turn. The death of Richter, among many deep feelings of sadness which it excites in me, affects me likewise with this very mean inconvenience, that I should and cannot give some more precise account of his life. The date of his death even is not known to me. This, however, surely might be learned.[1]

But with regard to Maler Müller I confess myself totally helpless. This Müller is a person whom I do not recollect having heard you mention. Maler (Painter) is the *agnomen* by which he is commonly designated, though he has two Christian names besides. Richter, Horn, and other *Aesthetic* gentlemen speak in high terms of him; and an intelligent Hamburger [2] whom I met with last summer recommends him with panegyrics almost rapturous. In short, I have come to regard this Maler Müller as an indispensable personage; and to believe that I cannot with a safe conscience present my Seven Champions of Germany to the English unless he be among the number. It seems he was a contemporary of Goethe in early days, and published various choice pieces about the period of *Werter;* but afterwards forsook poetry for painting, in the but moderately successful pursuit of which he died some months ago at Rome. His Literary works (Maler Müller's *Sämmtliche Werke*, 3 Bände, 8°) are mentioned in Fleischer's catalogue, as published at Heidelberg in 1811; since which time it would appear they have met with quite a new reception; and says my Hamburg correspondent, 'it is even thought that had he continued to cultivate poetry, he might have all but equalled Goethe himself!'

Forgive me these horrid blots, it is a chance to which the finest Calligrapher is exposed when his pen has been six weeks on duty and his ink become a syrup.

Now you can easily figure how gladly I would buy these three

[1] 14th November 1825.
[2] Dr. Julius. See *Early Letters of Carlyle*, Norton, 1887.

volumes; borrow them, beg them, nay, almost steal them; so any one of these four modes of appropriation could bring them into my hand. As I have no late catalogue of any London German Bookseller, it seems barely possible that Bonte, widow Boosey, Black, or some of these people may have the article in their possession. Nay, failing this, who knows but your Mrs. Aders or some other of your German friends may have it in their library, and be prevailed upon for the sake of helping a disconsolate Author out of this Slough of Despond, to let him have it for a week or two in his extreme need? If you can possibly do anything for me, I know you will do it; if not, why then we must just summon our Christian fortitude, and await in meekness and humility the chances of wind and weather. I will tell you again what I want:

(1) Hoffmann's (C. T. A.) *Leben und Nachlass*, or any account of his life, even the date of his decease.

(2) Richter's *Schmelzle* and *Quintus Fixlein* and the same thing about *his* life.

(3) Maler Müller's *Werke*, with, if possible, the like appendage.

The first of these works would enable me to go on for the matter of four weeks; by which time, it is likely enough, the Leipzig package may have arrived; the last would enable me in some measure to make ends meet without its arrival; the whole three would elevate me on the 'Rock of Necessity,' from which I might snap my fingers in the face of all chances whatsoever.

I confess, my dear Sir, I have very little hope that it will be in your power to accomplish aught for me in this difficulty: yet when I have tried you, I am at the very end of my resources; at which point, as you know, it is much easier to rest in patience than at any nearer one. So I trespass once more on your [good] [1] nature, still trusting, though feebly. If you succeed in getting any of these books, and can leave them with C. Tait, Bookseller, Sign of Horace's Head, 63 Fleet Street, he will send them directly to his brother in Edinburgh, who is my Bookseller in this adventure. The Fleet Street Tait will, of course, purchase, that is, pay the books, if purchasing or paying avail: but this I doubt much.

At all events I shall gain a letter from you, by this attempt I am making; and that will amply repay the trouble it costs me. I have not forgotten the still Temple, nor Alsatia, nor the kind Philosopher that dwells there. When you see this book, I hope

[1] Torn by seal.

you will find that your advices have not been quite thrown away
on me; and here and there a little trait will remind you of our
dialogues over coffee and *Sally Lunns*. I have a note about
Nicolai and *Philisters*, to which I would gladly have appended an
acknowledgment to the proper quarter, had I been authorized.

Literary news, news of yourself, news of all kinds, are a scarcity
with me here. For many months after leaving you I lay as if in
the Castle of Indolence; stretched under whispering beeches
reading German, smoking Orinocco, and one of the lordliest
prospects in the world spread out at my feet; Skiddaw, Saddle-
back, Helvellyn, and all these everlasting hills for my background,
the silver water of the Solway in front, my time slipped smoothly
away, divided into two portions like Lafontaine's *l'une se passait à
dormir, l'autre à ne rien faire*. I am grown a little healthier and
much happier, but I am still as recluded as ever. If you can
let me hear afar off the tumult of the Brick Universe, its sound
will be welcome to me; for there is much in your Babylon that
I like, and hope to revisit under kinder auspices. Believe me
always,

My dear Sir,
Most faithfully yours,
THOMAS CARLYLE.

I have a long row of Spanish books now in my eye; for which
my conscience many a time reproves me. I will send them when
I go to Edinburgh; sooner if you require them.

What has become of Coleridge and his book of *Aids*? Where
loiter the sweet singers of England, that no twang of a melodious
string is heard throughout the Isle, nothing but the chink of
yellow bullion? Alas! We are all Philistines together. But
veniet dies!

Edinburgh, 21 Comel[e]y Bank, 14th May 1827.

(3) My dear Sir,—May I beg of you to accept this copy of my
last Compilation in the furtherance of which you more than once
showed yourself so ready to assist with *Rath und That*; a service
which I would willingly convince you that I have not forgotten,
however unable to do more than remember it. The Book has
been out for some time, and your copy should have been sent
sooner; but Late is better than Never; and I still hope you will
accept the little gift in good part, and sometimes think of me with
favour when you see it in your shelves.

I have got some Spanish books of yours, a *Don Quixote* and a

Quevedo, which I still keep in spite of the reproaches of my conscience, now really getting rather bored on the subject. The truth is the volumes are not by me at this moment, but in Dumfries-shire; and my only consolation is that they are safe, and that your need of them is not pressing. I am ashamed to say that I have yet read far too little of them, or indeed of any Spanish work, though some late German translations from that language (particularly one of Calderon) have not a little strengthened my wish to become immediately acquainted with it. One is so busy, so laboriously idle! It will be long before I write aught worth reading, and yet I must not let my pen grow altogether rusty, and so my reading is too much curtailed.

I have got wedded [1] since I wrote last: my wife also is a reader and a lover of German; and we have a pleasant cottage here with China roses and the like, and the towers of Edinburgh peering through the branches of our *tree*, at a safe distance. Would not the best way to get your books be to come hither in vacation time and seek them? I am sure it would be the surest; and we could form as pretty a *bureau d'intelligence* for the discussion of *aesthetic* matters here, as you would wish to see. There is a spare bed, too, and coffee worthy of King's Bench Walk itself. Oh, I would give a shilling to see one other Sally Lunn! But the Temple with its reverend alleys, and good inmates, is become a reminiscence; and London, huge, monstrous London itself, looks beautiful by distance. Surely I shall once more see it, and the chosen men that make it worth seeing.

A letter from you, full of news of all sorts, would be a treat to be remembered. Some sultry noon, when your streets approach the first degree of Wedgwood, and you cannot stir abroad, for being broiled, who knows but you may favour me? I really should receive it as a most kind service. At all events if I can assist you in aught here, or in *any* way manifest my sense of obligation to you, I shall *expect* to be applied to.

Believe me always, my dear Sir,
Most faithfully yours,

T. CARLYLE.

I have more than once meditated inquiring of you about that 'London University,' of yours. I learn from the Newspapers that the people have advertised for Professors; but never having seen the advertisement itself, the offers they have made, the persons to be applied to, in short, the whole aspect of this matter

---

[1] 17th October 1826.

is unknown to me.   If you know, or can learn aught throwing light on it, I should be thankful to hear you; for certain of my friends are clear that I should make application for a post in that new Seminary; and, indeed to myself it seems that some Moral Philosophy or Rhetoric Professorship there would be no such unhandsome appointment.   I can teach Mathematics also, and Physics (Physic, alas! I know practically) and touches of Metaphysics, the oddest mixture of Scotch and German, Dugald Stewart and Immanuel Kant!   But the fittest place for me would be that of 'Jack of all Trades,' in case they wanted such a hand. Seriously I should like to know.

[Endorsed on letter by Crabb Robinson:]

14th May 1827 (received June).   Carlyle with German book.

1864.   The now famous Thomas Carlyle.

The book here mentioned and given to me was the first of his numerous works.   Our acquaintance has long ceased.

APPENDIX II

[By permission of Miss Emma Hutchinson]

(1) JULY 4th 1850. [A leaflet about the meeting at Justice Coleridge's which resolved to raise a subscription to do honour to the memory of Wordsworth and determined the objects of the subscription. It gives the names of the Committee and of the Executive Sub-committee and a preliminary list of subscribers. On the back is a letter to John Miller, written from Bury. Crabb Robinson says he is on the sub-committee *not* by his own act.]
. . . I here content myself with saying that Dr. Chr. Wordsworth is now at Rydal, preparing under Mrs. Wordsworth's eye a memoir of our departed friend, and that *The Recluse*, part one, is to appear forthwith. . . . In the 5th volume of Southey's *Life*, there is a brief notice of our old friend E[lton] H[amond] but without anything to betray his name, and indeed very little to draw attention to the fact.

(2) DEC. 1st 1850.

(3) OCT. 4th 1852. . . . There comes into play a sentiment which dear Charles Lamb felt intensely and expressed as he did every[thing] with an enriching humour. I carried him an invitation to drive with a common friend. 'There will be only the three Stansfelds.' 'How I *hate* those three Stansfelds.' 'Hate them! Why, they are three Yorkshiremen. You have never seen *one* of them.' 'That's the reason! I cannot hate any one I have ever seen.' I used to say to Charles Lamb: 'I will adopt your pets, but not your antipathies.' . . .

(4) NOV. 24th 1852.

(5) JAN. 14th 1853. . . . The better half of this letter . . . consists of a copy and remarks on the most marvellous poem [*The Bridge of Sighs* by T. Hood] I have met with of late years. . . .
. . . Of all the men of genius I ever knew, Charles Lamb was the one I most intensely loved.—My love proves nothing, but he was loved with equal warmth coupled with like admiration by

Thomas Clarkson and his wife, my dear friend; by Southey, Coleridge, Wordsworth, etc. . . .

(6) [Undated but placed here by contents.]

(7) APRIL 1st 1853. . . . In your estimate of the *Bridge of Sighs*—disappointing title by the bye, and therefore to be regretted—I ally concur, even in censures which I would not have brought forward, but being uttered by you, or indeed any one, could not remove or contradict. Tho' as I am afraid, I have already said oftener than necessary, that I am infinitely more obliged to the critic who points out to me a beauty I might not have detected, than to him who makes me aware of a blemish I might have overlooked. Yet do not suppose me so *excessively* unwilling to see faults that I do not willingly receive and confess to be just, all the faults you find in Hood's marvellous poem. Far from it. I go further and think you have omitted just matter of reproach. . . . I agree with you that the *liberties* taken with the grammatical construction are excessive. The four lines commencing with 'Still for all slips of hers' want what is worse, I fear, than a grammatical construction—a logical connection. Why the lips are to be wiped 'for all slips' I do not see, and I have occasionally omitted those lines when reading. You have justly shown the *abuse* of the triple rhyme, and demanded for Wordsworth the preference to which he is entitled. . . .

. . . . Wordsworth himself in terms said that he thought he had more cause of complaint against the *Quarterly* than the *Edinburgh*. We can more easily forgive the open, rather ostentatious enemy, than the would-be-thought friend. . . .

(8) OCT. 10th–17th 1853. . . . A very amiable woman,[1] a *Calvinistic Dissenter*, who admiring the author nevertheless would not let her boys read it [*Mrs. Leicester's School*] till she had torn out *The Young Mahometan* and *The Witch Aunt*. When I told Lamb of this, he said: 'I am delighted to hear it; I wrote them both.' . . .

. . . As to Valentine Le Grice, I know a great deal more about him than I could bring within the compass of a letter. He is a remarkable man and so was his father before him. A native of my native town. . . . Val Le Grice is a strange man, one of those very clever unmanageable beings characterised in a couplet:

> And some there are blessed with huge stores of wit
> Who want as much again to manage it.[2]

[1] Mrs. Pattisson.
[2] For whan a man hath over greet a wit,
Full oft hym happeth to mysusen it.
> Chaucer, *Canon Yeoman's Prologue*, ll. 648–9.

I have heard Lamb tell odd stories about Le Grice, of whom the best to be said is that he overflowed with kindness to his fellow creatures, and was warm-hearted. He and Lamb loved each other, but Lamb confessed that he saw him ever with apprehension. And well he might.—They used to go to debating societies together—the same which I frequented years afterwards, and there made some of my most valuable friendships. They attended when the question was: *Who is the greatest orator, etc. ?* Le Grice rose: 'I was once in company, Mr. Chairman, when a lady was asked which she liked best, veal, mutton, or beef. She answered: Pork. So, sir, your question asks: *Who is the greatest orator, Burke, Pitt, or Fox ?* I answer *Sheridan.*' Another time on rising he said: 'Mr. Chairman, the last time I entered this room, I had the honour to be kicked out of it.' 'I was present,' said Lamb, 'and certainly he deserved it.' . . .

[PS.] . . . Mrs. Wordsworth is here at Henry Taylor's. She does not know you personally, but as the friend of her nephew, desires to be kindly remembered. We shall be going soon, that is in November, to see Mrs. Clarkson, the widow of the Slave-trade abolisher.

Mrs. Wordsworth is in good health apparently and is making a visit to a dear friend, Miss Fenwick—two pious women who consider this is a solemn leave-taking. She will, in my oldest friend Mrs. Clarkson, see one of her most esteemed friends. She will not go to see the statue [of the poet] in the artist's studio. . . .

(9) Nov. 22nd 1856. . . . What I love myself I am most anxious that all those I esteem should love also, considering love and enjoyment as the same. This led me to be a sort of martyr (I incurred the martyrdom of ridicule) in the cause of Wordsworth, but I have been amply rewarded by witnessing in old age the triumph of his poetical school. . . .

(10) SEPT. 3rd 1857.   Bury St. Edmunds.
My dear Sir,—It will give you pleasure, I have no doubt, to read that on a recent visit to Rydal I found dear Mrs. Wordsworth all I could wish and more than I could hope. It would seem burlesque to refer in speaking of a blind old woman of 88 to such an image as the *phantom of delight*, yet the weightier couplet:

> A perfect woman, nobly planned
> To warn, to comfort, and command,

may still be brought to one's mind.

In her extreme old age she has attained an age not contemplated in those three stanzas to which I have referred, and

exhibits a phase of existence worthy to be the sequel of those.—
I spent nearly a week with her. During my stay I had frequent
walks with her on the well-known terrace and read to her from
her husband's poems—the reading in which she most delights.

During this stay, I never heard a syllable of regret pass her
lips. She is the *beau ideal* of resignation. I probably related to
you an anecdote. It is said that at the very last moment of *his*
life, she was heard to whisper in his ear, 'You are going to Dora.'
We may be sure therefore that in her calm submission she never
forgets that she is going to William. The faithful James is still
at Rydal and will not leave his mistress. She had her choice
between her carriage and him and she retains him. She enjoys
the perfect health of an octogenarian.

Not far from Rydal resides Mrs. Hutchinson and her daughters.
They all speak of you with gratitude and affection as the friend and
patron of their son and brother, the clergyman, and are expecting
from his Northern Mission the other brother.

The chief changes I remark in this district are made by death.
Those who depart have successors, but in the nature of things
these must be for the present at least, *inferiors*, whatever they
may become hereafter. The most remarkable of the residents is
Mrs. Fletcher. . . . Mrs. Fletcher, older than Mrs. Wordsworth,
has been eulogised by Lord Brougham with his characteristic
force, and after years of comparative poverty and threatened with
want, she became the leader of Edinburgh literary society, but in
the time of Jeffrey's triumph was the almost single avowed admirer of the *Lyrical Ballads*. She exhibits the remains of great
personal beauty, resembling Mrs. Barbauld, in whose house I
saw her sixty years since.

There, too, is the widow of Dr. Arnold. She scarcely belongs
to the same *age*—yet she has a son known as the author of a
military novel of which the scene is in India. He is the head of
the Educational Establishment in the Punjab, and Mrs. Arnold
read to me a letter written early in the spring, before any outward
symptom was exhibited of the catastrophe that has since burst out,
in which, however, his apprehensions are clearly announced, and
now assume the character of prophecy. Subsequent letters from
him show that he is aware of the full extent of the peril, tho' it
has not yet reached the district in which he lives. . . .

(11) JAN. 12th 1858. . . . You are aware probably that the
placing of the Wordsworth monument has given great disgust
to a large proportion of the most zealous promoters of the

subscription. . . . The Queen gave £50 on condition that the monument to William Wordsworth should be placed in the Abbey. Nevertheless the Dean and Chapter extracted the full fee, as if the party represented had been a calico printer or Indian nabob. The precise sum I cannot now remember, but it was several hundred pounds—while the fee was remitted to those who placed Campbell's monument, I suppose in recognition of his higher merit! This is not all, but I have said more than enough.

I should like to know your opinion of the *new edition*. Your friend Mr. Johnston has had the advantage of connecting his own name honourably with that of the poet as Editor. . . .

(12) JUNE 4th [1858].

APPENDIX III

The following seventeen letters from Crabb Robinson to Samuel Naylor, junior, are in the possession of S. Naylor's granddaughter, Mrs. Clifford Bax, who has allowed me to see and make extracts from them:

Jan. 1st 1851	March 8th 1854
April 19th 1851	Dec. 11th 1854
Oct. 30th 1851	June 29th [1855]
Jan. 27th 1852	Sept. 14th [1855]
Aug. 5th [1852]	Nov. 21st 1855
Sept. 8th 1852	March 26th 1859
Nov. 16th [1852]	Dec. 28th 1859
Dec. 25th 1852	June 23rd 1869
Oct. 14th [1853]	

The years of the undated letters are proved by internal evidence.

(1) JAN. 1st 1851. . . . I need no motive beyond the mere love of excitement. Therefore I never suffer ennui. I shall be glad to hear that you can find as I can in mere reading a sufficient zest. To me the periodicals would supply almost enough of excitement. . . . Let me direct your attention to *Fraser's Magazine* . . . and in the year 1849 you will find some very clever papers entitled *Yeast*, a sort of novel—very like in character and perhaps better in execution than *Alton Locke*. The author is Kingsley, who fluctuates between sentimental religion and free-thinking. On leaving your house I fell in with the younger J. W. Parker, of West Strand, the publisher of *Fraser*—a clever young man. He, like Kingsley, etc., being trained in the Church school has broke bounds without being expelled the school. He belongs to an anomalous set, of which Julius Hare, Frederick Maurice, etc., are individuals. . . .

(2) SEPT. 8th 1852. . . . Here [Rydal] I came on Monday—intending to lie by as much as possible during the week I meant to spend here. But yesterday I could not help walking about eight

miles *not* to see the fine lake of Grasmere or the sweet Rydal Water
—here the scenery has always been subordinate to social feelings.
And the loss of the great poet, to which has been added that of his
son-in-law, Quillinan, renders this place in a great degree a place
for mournful recollections.   And here I have three most interesting persons all sharing my feelings concerning the departed, with
whom I spend my time: Mrs. Wordsworth, Mrs. Arnold, Mrs.
Fletcher, each in her own way most admirable.   Mrs. Fletcher, in
her eighty-third year, has the most vigorous nature of them
all. . . .

I envy you the pursuit of fine art.   It is that portion of it
especially which you cultivate, which I am least incapable of
relishing as it deserves—the art which in its highest form of
excellence gives

> To one brief moment caught from fleeting time
> The appropriate calm of blest Eternity.

Ruskin thanked me for communicating this sonnet to him.   I
have conceived a very high opinion of this man, and am quite
disturbed by his avowed disesteem of the greatest of landscape
painters, if this be a correct announcement of his highest function
—Claude Lorraine. . . .

(3) DEC. 25th 1852. . . . Mr. Rogers is now at Brighton.   He is
in his ninety-first year, and though a marvellous man in his way,
yet no one now asks anything of him, beyond the repetition of an
oft-repeated anecdote or joke.   In several instances, and some more
than a year ago, he undertook to do something which might be
fairly expected of him, and from the not doing of which a loss was
sustained in a cause in which he took an interest.   But he forgot
what he was to do, though the person to whom he was to speak
was often at his elbow! . . .

(4) DEC. 11th 1854. . . . Of literature I have nothing to say
within a writable or even readable compass.   And yet there is
much that is curious abroad.   The most remarkable books now
coming out are the collection of De Quincey's writings.   Even
his diseased malice cannot altogether take away the charm of his
writings. . . .

APPENDIX IV

EXCERPT FROM LETTER OF CRABB ROBINSON TO J. P. COLLIER

[By permission of Mr. R. W. Gibson, Antiquarian Bookseller, Oxford]

Nov. 26th 1856. . . . I found on my table 5 vols. to be read—all new.—Yours [1] excites the most interest both on account of the author and the subject. I expect great pleasure from half of yours. The portion assigned to a reprint I pass over.—The Preface I must not speak of unread, but as I presume it is controversial and in self-vindication, I wish it unwritten, for even the successful defence implies the having suffered injustice. . . .

[1] *Seven Lectures on Shakespeare and Milton by the late S. T. Coleridge. A List of All the MS. Emendations in Mr. Collier's Folio, 1632; and an Introductory Preface.* 1856.

APPENDIX V

[*By permission of Mr. Martin Hardie*]

Pattisson Correspondence

Volume 1, 1629–1805

(1) To Mrs. Jacob Pattisson, senior. Colchester, 6th April 1795.
H. C. Robinson has sent Mrs. Pattisson [1] a round Dozen of Novels
besides a Catalogue which Mrs. Pattisson will either purchase or
return when she sends a Parcel as she thinks proper. Out of the
List which Mrs. P. sent (which H. C. R. always carries in his
Hand and selects from it as many Books as he can find) H. C. R.
could only catch

The Emigrants. 3 vols.[1]
Family Party. 3 vols.[2]

In order to complete a Parcel he has sent

Theagenes and Chariclea. 2 vols.[3]

which, in the Law Phrase, he Warrants Excellent, and recommends
to Mrs. P.'s particular Attention.—And

Mrs. Inchbald's *Simple Story*. 4 vols.

which was considered as a Work superior to Common Novels by
the Reviewers. H. C. R. would have selected some Novels he
read about 7 years ago, but he was fearful that he might pitch
upon those Mrs. P. had read. He recollects *The Fool of Quality* [4]
was then esteemed an eccentric Work. And *Arundel* [5] was lately
recommended to him by a Young Woman of very distinguished
Talents, Amelia Alderson [Opie] as a work of first-rate Merit.

---

[1] *The Emigrants, A Gallic Tale.* 1794.
[2] 1791. Both these novels are mentioned in the *New Annual Register*.
[3] By Heliodorus. *An Æthiopian History*, translated by T. Under-
downe. 1587. A fresh translation, anonymous, appeared in 1791.
[4] By Henry Brooke. 1766.
[5] By Richard Cumberland. 1789.

There are several Modern Novels which are now all the 'rage'—

Madeline.[1]
The Weird Sisters.[2]
The Cyprists.[3]

which perhaps Mrs. P. might desire to see, but H. C. R. cannot recommend them himself as he has not during some Months read any Work of the kind.   H. C. R. takes the Liberty of reminding Mrs. P. that Johnson's *Rasselas* and the Continuation of it called *Dinarbas* [4] rank highly in this Species of Composition. . . .

(2) To William Pattisson.   Colchester, 4th May 1795.

. . . I suppose you have not yet seen *The British Critic* of the last Month which has reviewed the first Vol. of the *Cabinet*. [Here follows a summary of the criticisms which 'were in direct opposition to ours' as regards the essays, one by Charles Marsh. Crabb Robinson proceeds to give his own opinion on the various poems in the *Cabinet*, some of which he thinks 'would not disgrace Della Crusca.']

(3) To W. P.   25th April 1795.
[Consists in the main of an essay on *The Profession of a Barrister*, Section I: *Morality as a Principle of Action*.   In a marginal commentary Crabb Robinson writes:] I claim no Originality of Idea. The greatest part of the reasoning is derived from Godwin and is an abridgement of his Morality; tho' I admit that my Ideas were received from him, I ought to observe that nothing has been taken from him *verbatim*.   And tho' I had made an Analysis of the 1st vol. I did not refer to it when I wrote this Letter.   There is also one point in which I differ totally from Godwin and he would be very severe upon the first part of my Letter.   Godwin established the Origin of Moral Duty upon a Principle of Disinterestedness natural to Man (which by the bye appears to me consummate Nonsense.)   He does not call to his Assistance a future State and is very severe upon the Self Love system.

(4) To W. P.   9th May 1795.
[2nd section of same essay: *On the Study of the Law*.]

(5) To W. P.   Bury, 24th August 1795.
[3rd section of same essay: *On the Practice of the Bar*.]

[1] By Isabella Kelley.   3 vols.   1794.
[2] 3 vols.   1794.   *New Annual Register*.
[3] 2 vols.   1795.   *New Annual Register*.
[4] *Dinarbas, a Tale, being a continuation of Rasselas*, by Ellis Cornelia Knight.   1790.

Volume 2, 1795–6

(6) To Mrs. J. Pattisson.   Colchester, 8 March 1795.

(7) To W. P.   Colchester, 26 May 1795.

. . . I will like a Knight Errant of the Days of Chivalry main-
tain that the fair beautiful and peerless System of Godwin is
superior to all other systems. And I will defend with my Sword
and Buckler its incomparable Worth. . . .

(8) To W. P.   Bury, 17th November 1795.
Dear Pattisson,

Without scruple I confess that I wrote *Philo-Godwin*. I
thought you would have discovered me before, for I had written
it when you were in Bury, but as it had not then appeared in the
Cambridge Intelligencer I kept it a secret. . . . I bar your excepting
to a very obscure Passage where I had compared Paine with
Godwin and where the Printers by omitting a Line converted a
decent Parallel into Nonsense. . . .

Volume 3, 1797–1800

(9) To W. P.   Savile Row, 29th September 1797.

On Friday I began *Ossian*. I am indeed charmed [?]
extremely beyond Expectation and considerably beyond Measure
with his poems. At present *Carthor* is my favourite. . . .

(10) To W. P.   Bury, 3rd May 1798.

(11) To W. P.   Bury, 31st May 1798.

(12) To Thomas Amyot.   Bury, 3rd July 1798.

(13) To W. P.   Bury, 31st July 1798.

(14) To W. P. and to Mrs. Newton. Yarmouth, 8th Sept. 1798.

(15) To W. P.   London, 31st October 1798.

(16) To W. P.   London, 22 November 1798.
[Defence of Burke's consistency.]

(17) To W. P.   London, 19th February 1799.

. . . Of modern Literature I have nothing interesting to say
but that Mackintosh has published an Introduction to a course of
Lectures on the Law of Nature and Nations. It is one of the
most exquisite Morsels both in Sense and Style that I have ever
seen. . . .

(18) To W. P.   London, 27 June 1799.

(19) To W. P.   Devizes, 9th December 1799.

(20) To Mrs. W. P.   Devizes, 16 March 1800.

Volume 4. 1797–1831

(21) To W. P.   Bury, 26th March 1798.

(22) To W. P.   Bury, 22nd April 1798.

. . . I am labouring through *Zoonomia*,[1] which is too unlike the Books I have been used to read to be easy or pleasant, particularly the more medical chapters. I have re-perused *The Mysteries of Udolpho* with Delight. . . .

(23) To W. P.   Bury, 18th May 1798.

(24) To W. P.   Bury, 14th February 1800.

(25) To W. P.   Grimma, 20th December 1801.

(26) To W. P.   Frankfurt, 6th July 1802.

(27) To W. P. and Mrs. W. P.   Jena, 25th October 1802.

(28) To W. P. and Mrs. W. P.
           Hatton Garden, 31st January 1813.

. . . I have no doubt you have good nature enough to be pleased with the success of Coleridge's Tragedy.[2] It is by no means probable that it will attain so advanced an old age as till your visit, but if it do, I shall use all my entreaties with you and William to go and see it. . . .

(29) To W. P. and Mrs. W. P.   13th December 1816.

(30) To W. P.   Bury, 13th April 1817.

(31) To W. P. and Mrs. W. P.   Rome, 27th December 1830.

Volume 5. 1802–4

(32) To W. P.   Jena, 7th May 1803.

(33) To Mrs. W. P.   London, 3rd December 1806.

Volume 6. 1805–6

(34) To W. P.   Bagshot, 22nd December 1805.

. . . Miss Hays lives in retirement, an highly respected character. She pursues literature as a profession; she does not estimate her productions above their value; she is content to be a useful writer and does not lose feminine excellence and virtues while she seeks literary fame. . . . I dined . . . with Mrs. Barbauld and to my admiration of her as a writer there is now associated a great personal regard for her. She is altogether without

---

[1] By Erasmus Darwin.   [2] *Remorse.*

pretension and at the same time without the affectation of modesty which I should censure more.   She speaks with decision and discrimination. . . . Dr. Aikin is a man of sharp understanding, but still, compared with his sister, he is in company what his Writings are compared with hers. . . .

(35) To Mrs. W. P.   Bury, 12th February 1806.
                                         [Misdated 1867.]

(36) To W. P. and Mrs. W. P.   London, 4th April 1806.
   . . . I have been twice at Mrs. Barbauld's . . . and have every encouragement from her and Mr. B. to renew my visits.   They both interest me exceedingly.   I have seen her shew off.   She reasons acutely tho' that is not her great excellence.   The *suaviter in modo* is most peculiarly hers.   She has the *fortiter in re* but in common with other superior persons of our Age.   There is something repulsive in Dr. Aikin. . . . Lucy Aikin is the only member of the family I do not like.   Every other person in it is on the whole amiable and interesting, for the something I have objected to in the Doctor, does not outweigh the conviction of his sense and integrity which every one will be persuaded of who sees the Doctor. . . .

(37) To W. P. and Mrs. W. P.   London, 5th August 1805.

(38) To W. P.   [torn edge] November 1806.

Volume 7.   1807–9

(39) To W. P.   Altona, 24th March 1807.

(40) To W. P.   London, 21st November 1807.
   . . . I have looked into W. Hazlitt's answer to Malthus.   It is rich in good things without being itself a good thing.   It is acute, but pert; argumentative, but the argument is directed more against unessential parts of the book he writes against than against the system itself.   It has not changed my opinion in the least as to the great question, tho' it has given great force and clearness to a number of correcting and qualifying remarks which had before occurred to me.   There are many very light and censurable things in it, yet it is an amusing book.   The concluding 2 pages is a piece of masterly eloquence.
   I can at the same time recommend, however, another book of Hazlitt's from which you will all . . . receive great pleasure.   It is his Abridgement of Tucker's *Light of Nature*, 1 vol. 8vo.[1]   The preface has some of the best remarks I have ever seen on Kant's

---

[1] *The Light of Nature Pursued*, by Abraham Tucker.

philosophy. Tucker's book itself is very curious indeed. I have read the *Vision*, which in spite of its oddities, is highly interesting. . . .

(41) To H. Pattisson.   London, 24th November 1817.
   [Incomplete]

(42) To W. P.   London, 1st January 1808.

(43) To W. P.   London, 5th January 1808.

(44) To W. and H. P.   London, 14th April 1808.

 . . . If you want books I can with confidence recommend *Plymley's Letters*.[1] They will delight you, for they are on the right side and are written with great talent and humour. Since the barbarous Gothamite taste you betray in matters of poetry, I despair [*sic*] must deprive you of all interest in the persons of my favourite Poet[s], I shall only say in general that I have made the acquaintance of Wordsworth. He is an highly interesting man and has confirmed me in all my previous notions of the close connection of high moral excellence and the poetic character. I had long conversations with him on the subject of poetry and I wish I could be with you for a week were it only to deliver a few lectures to you on a subject which would interest me. I have also seen Southey and have been asked by Coleridge to go and see him. You see I am in with all of them. . . .

(45) To H. P.   London, 21st May 1808.

(46) To W. and H. P.   Corunna, 31st August 1808.

(47) To H. P.   London, 5th April 1809.

 . . . You may if you please think Locke a great metaphysician and Pope a great Poet, you may laugh in your ignorance at Kant and refuse to understand and feel that Wordsworth has deep moral feeling and high poetic conceptions of man . . . and for all these heresies against good taste and sound philosophy I shall never be a whit displeased. . . . I am delighted that you are so much pleased with Miss Lamb's book. I shall give her your letter because it will give her pleasure. She is a very worthy woman indeed—a prime favourite with me as you know. . . .

(48) To W. P.   London, 8th May 1809.

 . . . Capel Lofft . . . tried late in the evening to gain a hearing in order to propose the memory of Charles James Fox, but he could not get a hearing. He was pathetic and implored attention, but all in vain. . . . I breakfasted with him yesterday at Richard

---

[1] By Sydney Smith.

Taylor's and have seen a great deal of him to-day also. I have had great pleasure in his company notwithstanding all his oddities. . . .

(49) To W. and H. P.　　　London, 19th November 1809.

. . . I am at this moment rather in a hippish mood, having just finished, 1 a.m., *Ennui*.[1] You have read this useful and moral Tale and can tell what chords within me it strikes rather harshly. . . .

Volume 8.　1810–11

(50) To H. P.　　　Bury, 2nd January 1810.

. . . Coleridge's last *Friend* contains 4 Sonnets[2] by Wordsworth, so noble that I am sure you would be converted to high admiration of him. Such real purity of moral sentiment, such heroic dignity of public feeling I never saw before clothed in poetic form so beautiful and exquisite. . . .

(51) To H. P.　　　London, 5th April 1810.

(52) To Mrs. Pattisson, senior.　　　London, 24th April 1810.

(53) To Mrs. W. P.　　　London, 5th June 1810.

(54) To W. P. and Mrs. W. P.　　　Bagshot, 25th July 1810.

(55) To Mrs. W. P.　　　London, 9th November 1810.

. . . In reference to my own work, I have to ask has William *The Diversions of Purley*?[3] If so, I can spare my trunk weight and room. . . .

(56) To W. P. and Mrs. W. P. London, 26th December 1810.

. . . There is generally a reciprocity of feeling. Love, esteem, friendship are mutual in most cases because they belong to the heart, while the opinion the judgment forms is self-subsistent. It does not follow that because I look upon any man, Coleridge for instance, as a genius that he must therefore think me a philosopher, tho' he will probably, if he is acquainted with my opinion, deem me a man of good sense and correct taste. Poor Coleridge! the name awakens a number of interesting reflections. How insufficient is mere genius for moral purposes, and what weakness and obliquity may not the finest and purest intellect permit the indulgence of, where the sedative of moral habits and severe

---

[1] By Maria Edgeworth.

[2] 'The land we from our fathers had in trust,' 'And is it among rude untutored dales,' 'O'er the wide earth, on mountain and on plain,' 'It was a *moral* end for which they fought.'

[3] By Horne Tooke.

principle are wanting! Coleridge dined with us on Sunday. He was the delight of a large party from half-past three till 12 o'clock. He discoursed of politics, metaphysics, and Shakespeare with equal brilliancy, yet I fear he will with all his infinite powers leave behind him no permanent record of a salutary exercise of his talents, unless he is to be considered, as perhaps the Greek philosophers were, a public instructor, a desultory educator of adults. And in this way he may, and I have no doubt does, scatter the seeds of wisdom wherever he appears.—But I know not how I have been led to digress on Coleridge. . . .

(57) To W. P. and Mrs. W. P.   London, 15th January 1811.

(58) To Mrs. W. P.   London, 16th April 1811.
    . . . I called yesterday on Mrs. Charles Aikin. She has promised to lend me *Thalaba* which she prefers to *Kehama*. . . .
    . . . I saw Godwin last night . . . Godwin by the bye, without being attached to any sect of Christians, as you may suppose, considers Sandeman as one of the most consistent of the leaders of parties. . . .

(59) To Jacob Pattisson.   London, 16th April 1811.

(60) To W. P. and Mrs. W. P.   London, 9th May 1811.

(61) To Mrs. W. P.   London, 23rd July 1811.
    . . . I will call at half-past ten in Newgate Street and I will thank you to give me or leave me *Thalaba* there. Of course I should be disappointed not to finish the poem on your return, but the volume need not lie unused during your absence. . . .

(62) To Mrs. W. P.   London, 27th August 1811.

(63) To W. P.   Bury, 23rd September 1811.

(64) To Mrs. W. P.   London, 18th December 1811.

(65) To Mrs. W. P.   Bury, 27th December 1811.

(66) To W. P.   Bury, [?] December 1811.

Volume 9.   1812–14

(67) To Mrs. W. P.   London, [?] February 1812.

(68) To Mrs. W. P.   London, 24th March 1812.
    . . . I have been with Mrs. Barbauld but twice within six months. . . . My evenings have been frequently spent in hearing lectures by Coleridge, Hazlitt, and Flaxman. . . .

(69) To Mrs. W. P.   London, 16th September 1812.
    . . . I think of Miss Baillie's plays as you do, and Ellis's

Specimens [1] are better qualified to instruct than give immediate pleasure. . . .

(70) To W. P. and Mrs. W. P.   London, 26th October 1812.

(71) To Mrs. W. P.   London, 21st January 1813.

. . . It will be a sad result of my late adoption of a profession . . . should I be forced to forgo that kind of literary pleasure in which you have so frequently sympathised with me. *A propos* of this better kind of the pleasures of taste, I will copy, without apology, a sonnet I lately met with in the *Courier*. I pity those who will not feel and appreciate it. [Here follows Wordsworth's sonnet: 'Now that all hearts are glad, all faces bright.']

(72) To Mrs. W. P.   London, 30th March 1813.

. . . I told Mrs. T[hornthwaite] when I wrote last, to recommend for your book-club Disraeli on the *Calamities of Authors*. It has very much amused me. . . . You will not suspect any *insidious* design on my part in praising it. I have never read a book which exhibits in a more impressive manner the 'follies of the wise.' It is a truly *moral* work and may be commended as a specific to all young people who are in danger of being seduced by the vain and meretricious attractions of literary glory. . . .

(73) To Mrs. W. P.   London, 7th April 1813.

(74) To Mrs. W. P.   London, 5th May 1813.

(75) To Mrs. W. P.   Bury, [?] July 1813.

. . . I ought to have acknowledged the kind loan of Burns before. . . .

(76) To W. P. and Mrs. W. P.   Bury, 13th October 1813.

(77) To Mrs. W. P.   London, [2] [no date, P.M. 1813.]

. . . I shall be glad indeed to introduce you to Mrs. Barbauld. . . . You may tell me all you think and feel and all you love and hate in Madame de Staël without any fear of wounding any tender part about me. My admiration of her is great but very far indeed from being unqualified. . . . But nothing in her or her works fixes my love and admiration as the works of the Northern Poet continue to do. . . .

(78) To W. P.   Jena, 7th February 1804.

. . . I have discovered with great pleasure that our favourite Dr. Aikin and Mrs. Barbauld are worthy pupils of the Horatian School. Dr. Aikin indeed has not the delicate taste or sportive

---

[1] George Ellis. *Specimens of Early English Metrical Romances.* 1805.
[2] From internal evidence.

fancy of his Master.   But Mrs. Barbauld has added a new charm
to the genuine Horatian grace of her mind and pencil by the gentle
corrections and qualifications arising from the purer and juster
morals of Christianity.   By adding to the sober wisdom and
chaste pleasantry of the Roman (of course I do not refer to the 8th
and 12th Epodes [*sic*], etc.) the hopes and humane sentiments of
Christianity, she has, if I may use the phrase, sanctified Horace.
. . .

(79) To W. P. and Mrs. W. P.   London, 15th February 1814.

Volume 10.   1814–16

(80) To Mrs. W. P.   Bury, 27th July 1814.

(81) To W. P.   Paris, 25th September 1814.
. . . I visit Helen Maria Williams. . . .

(82) To W. P.   London, 8th December 1814.

(83) To W. P. and Mrs. W. P.   London, 6th February 1815.
. . . My last Witham visit was in no respect uncomfortable and
the want of an entire sympathy in regard to the Poet and the Poem [1]
only served to stimulate to a salutary exercise of reasoning and—
forbearance. . . . To-day I received a letter from your friend Mr.
Fox [2] of Chichester.   He had indirectly applied to me for information about German books.   I wrote to offer him the use of mine
and I mentioned my late reading of the Poem to Hannah.   In
return he speaks of Wordsworth in terms of praise so discrimi-
nating that a friend of W.'s has taken the letter away to copy a
part of it.   I am satisfied with the progress the work is making.
Half of the impression is already sold.   You will be interested
perhaps to hear that Montgomery is author of the *Eclectic* article.
This Josiah Conder informed me, who is now the Editor of the
review.   I am glad that Montgomery did write that review.   It
is pleasing to observe free and even exuberant eulogy from a
rival, who might be sooner than another tempted to 'damn with
faint praise.'   Hannah [Mrs. W. H. Pattisson] will further be
amused by hearing that I have heard of Hogg, the author of the
Queen's Wake.   He has been visiting Wordsworth, who entertains
great respect for his talents.   Hogg is, like Burns, a genuine
peasant.   But he is prudent.   With all his simplicity of character and habits, still a Scotchman in the main.   He thinks

[1] *The Excursion.*
[2] William Johnson Fox.   The letter is No. 121 of the 1809–17 volume
of Crabb Robinson's correspondence.

Jeffrey the greatest living writer, and the late *Edinburgh* review of his work appears to have been an exchange of eulogy. Further I have to inform you that I have seen a proof sheet of Wordsworth's new edition of his Poems. It will be a very *beautiful* work as to its outward form and substance. He has condescended to *adorn* many of his poems, but has sturdily refused to *exclude* any one.

I hear from everyone so high a character of Southey's *Don Roderick*,[1] that I think you may venture to buy it for your bookclub: on the other hand, *The Lord of the Isles* is less talked of than I expected. The fact undoubtedly is that Lord Byron has put Scott's nose out of joint—and no wonder, for what is popularity but a system of favouritism? Possibly Scott's concealment of himself, if he be really the author of *Waverley*, is a prudent policy. Wordsworth, I hear, is a great admirer of *Waverley*, and he ascribes it also to Scott. . . .

My love to [the boys] when you write. I have been buying for them Miss Edgeworth's *Moral* and *Popular Tales*. . . . Perhaps with your usual precaution you may like to read them first. I would recommend *Forester* and *L'Amie Inconnue* as very excellent; but I think the moral of both somewhat equivocal. However, it is not the sort of doubtful morality you will censure. . . .

(84) To Mrs. Pattisson, senior.　　[No date or address] 1815.

(85) To W. P. and Mrs. W. P.　　London, 16th April 1815.

. . . I have, since I began this letter, been looking into the new edition of Wordsworth's Poems. There are two new Prefaces and a great number of new pieces. Wordsworth has done me the *honour*, and I truly feel it as such, to send me a copy of the work, in which I shall take a heightened and extended delight. But I have been so busy for these few days that I hardly know what the fresh treat amounts to. I have read some half dozen admirable sonnets on politics. . . .

(86) To W. P. and Mrs. W. P.　　Amsterdam and The Hague,
　　　　　　　　　　　　　　　　　　20th August 1815.

(87) To W. P. and Mrs. W. P.　　Bagshot, 4th October 1815.

(88) To W. P. and Mrs. W. P.　　London, 8th April 1816.

(89) To Mrs. W. P.　　Keswick, 17th September 1816.

[Consists of a detailed account, taken almost verbatim from his journal, of his visit with Torlonia and Walter to Rydal, and to

---

[1] *Roderick, the last of the Gothes*, by Southey, was published in 1814; Scott's *Vision of Don Roderick* had appeared in 1811.

Southey at Keswick, and of his own return to Rydal and journey with Wordsworth to Cockermouth, Calder Abbey, Ravenglass, and Eskdale.]

Volume 11. 1817–18

(90) To W. P. and Mrs. W. P.   London, 20th February 1817.

(91) To Mrs. W. P.   London, 8th May 1817.

. . . I take for granted you know that Talfourd is now a licensed special pleader. . . . Perhaps he is a little anxious about his success. I wish it were in my power to assist him. . . . I believe T. to be a very competent pleader. . . . It is much easier to recommend and bring forward a pleader than a barrister. . . .

(92) To W. P.   [? London], 20th June 1817.

(93) To Mrs. W. P.   London, 4th July 1817.

(94) To W. P.   London, 5th July 1817.

(95) To Mrs. W. P.   Bury, 27th March 1818.

(96) To Mrs. W. P.   Frankfurt, 15th September 1818.

(97) To Mrs. W. P.   Bury, 25th October 1818.

Volume 12. 1819–20

(98) To Mrs. W. P.   London, 1st February 1819.

. . . During my stay at Bury and on the Sessions journey I read a novel which pleased me very much indeed. If you have not read it I could recommend it to you confidently—*Pride and Prejudice*.[1] The merit lies in the perfect truth of the painting. The dialogue is exquisitely in character and the characters, tho' not ideal, are charming. The women especially are drawn after the life and Mrs. Bennet is a very jewel—equal to any of Ostade or Gerard Dou's portraits, and these you know are not prized for the beauty of the originals. Mr. Collins too, the sneaking and servile parson, is quite a masterpiece. The heroines (for there are a brace of them) are as natural as beauties can be and as beautiful as any successful portrait can be. . . . Since my return I have been reading, however, a still better book that you have probably already read—*The Heart of Midlothian*.[2] If not, read it directly. You were offended and with reason by the former *Tales of my Landlord*, for the tendency was not good certainly, tho' I think the author held up with perfect truth and impartiality at the same time the heroic virtue which religious feelings

[1] Published 1812.   [2] Published 1818.

produce, to our admiration, and the horrid crime to which religious fanaticism leads. But in this book he has made the *amende honorable* to the Scotch pietists or Cameronians. *Old douce David* may be put in comparison with the Reverend Mr. Primrose as a sort of Christian hero, and his exalted virtues are only thrown into relief by the human alloy. His narrow-mindedness and intolerance are rendered amusing only and excite no resentment in a character so scrupulously conscientious and upright. And I should have the lowest opinion of the understanding of a Unitarian who did not enjoy the fine characteristic speech in which *Socinian vermin* are spoken of with a contempt and horror quite boundless. Jeanie Deans too, the perfect heroine, loses none of our admiration because she, in the simplicity of her heart, doubts whether she can without sin enter a church where is an organ, or hear the word of God spoken by a man with a surplice on, and considers it as an 'awfu' thing' that there are so many prelatists in the city with the 'muckle kirk.' Swift said with truth, and I fear he was himself an instance, 'men have religion enough to hate and not enough to love each other,' and I think it one of the most laudable and useful of literary tasks to exhibit that excellence we all love and admire in combination with infirmities which we ought to learn to tolerate. This is not the only quality which renders this new *Tale of my Landlord* eminently moral. The conclusion of Effie Deans's history is very instructive. . . .

(99) To W. P.   London, 3rd March 1819.

(100) To W. P.   Bury, 26th April 1819.

(101) To W. P., junior.   [?] 1819.

(102) To W. P. and Mrs. W. P.   London, 31st October 1820.
   [Itinerary of tour with Wordsworth, etc.]
   . . . Such an excursion in fine weather and excellent company could not but be delightful, and I rejoice on reflection as I did while I was anticipating and actually partaking of the pleasures offered me. . . .

Volume 13.   1821–2

(103) To W. P.   London, 8th May 1822.

(104) To W. P.   London, 9th May 1822.

Volume 14.   1823–4

(105) To W. P.   London, 17th June 1823.

(106) To W. P.   London, 27th November 1824.

Volume 15.   1825–6

Nothing from Crabb Robinson.

Volume 16.   1827–30

(107) To W. P.   (Hannah's death.)   Bury, 20th July 1828.

(108) To W. P.   Bury, 3rd August 1828.

(109) To W. P.   Bury, 17th May 1829.

(110) To W. P.   Rome, 15th December 1829.

. . . In the same house is a very agreeable woman of a certain age, Miss Burney, sister of Madame D'Arblay, and herself the author of several esteemed novels. . . .

(111) To W. P. and sons.   Naples, 2nd April 1830.

(112) To W. P. and sons.   Florence, 17th July 1830.

[Asks for copies of *The Essays of Elia* and Coleridge's *Aids to Reflection* to be sent him.]

Volume 17.   1831–2

(113) To W. P. and sons.   Florence, 14th June 1831.

(114) To W. P. and sons.   Turin, 13th September 1831.

Volume 18.   1832–44

(115) To W. P.   London, 27th August 1837.

My dear friend,

I meant to send the accompanying Volumes long ago. But there has been blundering in their being forwarded to me. Mrs. Jacob Pattisson will find an autograph of the great poet in the last Volume. The Volumes of Lamb's letters will excite your pity as well as admiration, tho' Talfourd has shewn great skill in the throwing into shade what, in a prominent light, would have wounded the feelings of survivors and friends or provoked the sneers or reproaches of the unfriendly. Wordsworth says it is the only book of the kind he knows, executed with delicacy and judgment. Hereafter there may be large additions.—Mary Lamb, I rejoice to say, has been long in quiet good health. She shewed me her brother's grave a few days ago with composure and something like cheerfulness. . . .

(116) To J. P.   London, 19th June 1844.

Volume 19. 1845–50

(117) To Jacob P.   London, 22nd January 1846.

. . . I have heard Wordsworth speak very kindly both of the writings and person of Leigh Hunt. . . .

(118) To J. P.   Bury, 29th August 1846.

(119) To J. P.   London, 11th January 1847.

. . . I go to-morrow to Mr. Wordsworth (Rydal Mount, Ambleside) and mean to remain with him about three weeks. . . .

(120) To J. P.   Rydal, 1st January 1846.

. . . Here I have been enjoying myself in spite of very bad weather. There is congregated here a variety of talent and moral excellence quite astonishing in a place of so small population. To say nothing of the poet or any other males, the females alone form a singular delightful society. Here are Mrs. Wordsworth and her pious and benignant friend Miss Fenwick, and Mrs. Arnold, the worthy helpmate and survivor of the Doctor; Mrs. Fletcher, for many years the most distinguished member of Edinburgh society . . . and her two daughters, Mrs. Davy . . . and Miss Fletcher, also an authoress, and of recent accession, Harriet Martineau, who by her benevolence and generosity and activity of mind has conciliated the friendship of everyone in spite of Unitarianism and Mesmerism. . . .

(121) To J. P.   London, 17th January 184[9].

. . . I have begun to read Macaulay's very eloquent history. He has not abandoned the principles of political philosophy in which he was brought up, nor lost his love of civil and religious liberty. . . . You will be glad to hear that I found Mr. Wordsworth's mind in a much healthier state than it was last year. He has learnt to submit to the will of Providence in the loss of his daughter. Both he and Mrs. Wordsworth are in good health. . . .

(122) To J. P.   London, 22nd July 1847.

(123) To J. P.   Bury, 30th July 1850.

. . . My wish has been to be at Rydal. Mrs. Wordsworth has pressed my going to meet Miss Fenwick, and my intention is to go without losing a day the moment I am released from hence. . . .

(124) To J. P. (death of W. P.)   Leeds, 12th January 1848.

. . . Poor Wordsworth cannot bear up against the insupportable grief he feels for the death of his daughter. I was with him three weeks, during which time I was seldom able to withdraw his mind from the moody abstraction in which it seems to be from all

present objects.   This doubles Mrs. Wordsworth's affliction.   But
she is able to talk of this sorrow, the loss of her dear child. . . . I
will, however, tell you an anecdote of Wordsworth's man-servant
James, born a parish boy, who has lived all his days in servitude,
a *character* of whom I will one day tell you more.   Expressing my
sorrow that Mr. W. was unable to *submit*, he said: 'Ah, Sir, so I
took the liberty to say to him, and then master said: "Oh, but she
was such a bright creature."   And then I said: *"But don't you
think she is brighter now than she ever was?"*   And then he burst
into a flood of tears.'

These could not have been tears of unmixed grief.   But James's
answer may match with any to be found in the sayings of eminent
men. . . .

(125) To J. P.   London, 31st January 1848.

(126) To J. P.   London, 5th December 1847.

(127) To J. P.   Playford Hall, 20th September 1848.

(128) To J. P.   London, 28th March 1848.

[Of the French Revolution]

. . . I should despair but for a vague hope which clothes itself
in the words of our most spiritually-minded poets.   The last of
them has said that:

All things are less dreadful than they seem.[1] . . .

(129) To J. P.   London, 10th October 1850.

. . . I once said to Mrs. Arnold: 'I think your husband [2] was
one of the best Christians and worst Churchmen I ever knew.'
She smiled and said: 'There are many of that opinion.' . . .

. . . She [Mrs. Rutt] looked so venerable and so happy—'with
a sunny face' to borrow an epithet of Wordsworth's.[3] . . .

(130) To J. P.   London, 14th February 1848.

. . . I have been looking over the volume of letters [from himself to the Pattissons] this morning.—It is not like the volume
which I saw on Talfourd's drawing-room table—a bound collection of all the complimentary letters written on *Ion* and which
therefore it was intended everyone should read. . . . I am surprised
at the small number of letters from myself.[4] . . . There is no letter
between 1802 and 1813, nor between 1817 and 1830. . . .

[1] Wordsworth, *Ecclesiastical Sonnets*, Part I, sonnet VII, last line.
[2] Dr. Arnold of Rugby.
[3] Used of his neighbour, Mr. Harden.
[4] He continues in comment on some of these, notably on that dated
Rome, 27th December 1830 (number 31 in this list).

(131) To J. P.　　　　　　　　London, 22nd January 1848.

(132) To J. P.　　　　　　　　Bury, 9th July 1850.

. . . Having so little to say, I have thought it expedient to write on the back of the last circular [1] sent me, having a much greater number than I can distribute without the charge of obtru-[siveness], which there will not be from you under any circumstances and whether or not you rank your name among the admirers of the great Christian and moral poet. The subscription now, I understand, amounts to little more than £600 which will never suffice for a full length. Nor do I expect that the further subscriptions will be sufficient unless the Dean and Chapter remit the fee they usually demand for the licence to put up a full length—£300—which they probably will do out of respect to him. . . .

(133) To J. P.　　　　　　　　Bury, 6th September 1848.

. . . My brother is very comfortable in health but—
> By sudden blast or slow decline
> Our social comforts die away.

(134) To J. P.　　　　　　　　London, 4th May 1850.

. . . I did not go down to Westmorland to attend the funeral. Indeed the interment took place on the Saturday, and I should have scarcely had time. But I find I was expected and therefore I regret my absence. But in the first letter the time was not mentioned and I therefore inferred that I was not expected.

The grief of friends ought to be absorbed in the contemplation of the public loss, and yet the public of to-day will be the immediate gainers. There will be published forthwith THE POEM [2] which perhaps for the earnest and contemplative few of the present and future generations will be the most precious of the great man's works. In 14 books Wordsworth has recorded the formation of his character. This was written when his mind was in all its strength.

Dr. Christopher Wordsworth is commissioned to prepare brief memorials in illustration of his poems, and a short biography. I should have been better pleased had the task been given to Mr. Quillinan. For I fear there will be an inclination to press the great poet into the service of High Churchism. But this is not easy to do. There is at all events the sonnet *Young England* which is a bar in the way. Wordsworth henceforward will be classed with our English classics.

It will afford you satisfaction to know that Mrs. Wordsworth

---

[1] About the Wordsworth Memorial.　　　　　　[2] *The Prelude.*

has sustained this great trial as a Christian heroine should. She attended the funeral at which was a very large collection of the neighbours. This is the custom of the country. I am expected to go soon and I shall. . . . The notices of the public press have been creditable to the country['s] literature, at least as far as I have yet seen the papers. The best I have yet seen has been that of the *Inquirer*. I believe Mrs. Wordsworth will be gratified by it and acknowledge its Christian character though it is by a Unitarian. It is a curious fact that the Unitarians and the High Church have been among his warmest admirers. This power of uniting extremes in one common sentiment of love and admiration is an evidence of a *catholicity* of character. . . .

PS. I have had a letter from Mrs. Wordsworth since I wrote the above. She writes with great composure.

APPENDIX VI

THE following anecdotes, most of which have already been published either by Sadler or elsewhere, relate to men of letters:

No.
2. Horne Tooke.
6. Lamb (First Cause).
7. Hogg.
10. Rogers.
16. Ayrton. (Dirt-trumps.) Lamb not the author.
17. Lamb. (Luke-warm Christian.)
18. Lamb. (Compounds and simples.)
19. Lamb. (Shakespeare's anachronisms.)
35. Wordsworth. (Saul.)
36. Lamb. (Bacon and Cabbage.)
38. Capel Lofft.
42. Lamb. (Unitarians.)
47. Coleridge. (Bible Societies.)
48. Coleridge. (Goodness.)
50. Lamb. (Churchyard.)
51. Coleridge. (Bowyer.)
59. Lady Blessington. (Mrs. Norton's Wife.)
60. Sydney Smith. (Rogers.)
61. Mme. de Staël. (Coleridge.)
67. Coleridge. (Scotchmen.)
75. Coleridge. (Grapes and Gripes.)
77. Hood.
81. Porson. (Southey.)
88. Sydney Smith and Landseer.
92. Horne Tooke.
98. Theodore Hook.
99. Sydney Smith.
101. Theodore Hook. (Croker.)
102. Theodore Hook.
103. Theodore Hook.

No.

104. Theodore Hook.
107. Aikin.   (Cowper.)
108. Coleridge.   (Wordsworth.)
120. Sydney Smith.
123. Sydney Smith.
124. Sydney Smith.
127. Sydney Smith.
129. Disraeli.
140.[1] Disraeli.
141. Theodore Hook.
155. Tom Taylor.
156. Sydney Smith.
159. Kenyon.
160. Douglas Jerrold.
170. Coleridge.

[1] Should be 130.   The numbers are all ten out from here onwards.

APPENDIX VII

(This includes a List of Letters written to him by English Authors.)

I. WRITERS

CRABB ROBINSON'S correspondence and papers are preserved at Dr.
Williams's Library (i) in thirty-two volumes arranged chronologically,
and (ii) in eight Miscellaneous Bundles.

The following index is therefore twofold in its method. In the case
of the bound volumes, references are arranged in four columns which
give: (1) the date of the letter — this indicates the volume in which it
occurs, except where otherwise stated (e.g. 1848 in 1847 volume);
(2) the number of the letter in that volume; (3) the page of the letter;
(4) the number of the line in the page, unless it is the last, when it is so
designated, 'last seq.' means 'last line subject continued overleaf.' In
references to the Miscellaneous Bundles the actual letters or figures
given conform to the Library numbering which is not consistent. In
the index the first column gives the date of the letter without any indica-
tion where it may be found. The second column gives the number of
the bundle and letter in accordance with the Library procedure whatever
that may be (e.g. 3 A 32 is Bundle 3 A, letter 32; 2 IV K is Bundle 2,
subsection IV, letter K). The third and fourth columns, as in the case of
references to the bound volumes, contain information as to page and line
in the letter. It should further be noted that under the sub-heading
LETTERS, i.e. where reference is to the complete letter, the third and
fourth columns are ignored, and in cases in which more than one letter
occurs in any one year the references run on across the columns, thus:

$$1836 \quad 100; 134$$
$$1839 \quad 10; 19; 23; 26; 42;$$
$$49; 57; 69$$

The only references to Crabb Robinson's correspondence with the
Wordsworth family printed here are those found to have been accident-
ally omitted from *The Correspondence of Henry Crabb Robinson with the
Wordsworth Circle*, which contains a full index to the papers in this series
preserved at Dr. Williams's Library.

[ ] indicate information supplied by the editor.

( ) indicate a paraphrase in the text.

AGNEW, Eleanor C.			
Geraldine	1840	135	1	16
AGUILAR, Grace	1850	87	6	1
AIKIN, Anna Laetitia. *See* Barbauld, A. L.			

ALLSOP, Thomas—*contd.*

copies skit on Southey's verse by

  [Coleridge ?]   1866   77 *b*

  mentioned   1847   27   7   12

  WORK:

   Letters, Conversations, and Recol-

    lections of S. T. Coleridge   1865   24 *a*

  LETTERS to Crabb Robinson   1865   24 *a*

                           1866   60

Arabian Nights   1798   119   3   23

ARBLAY, Francis Burney, Mme D'. *See*

  D'Arblay

ARGYLL, Duke of. *See* Campbell, G. D.

ARNOLD, Matthew

  and family   1852   52   7   last

                       1856   21   4   25

               [in 1857 vol.]

                     1857   30 *a*   4   10

  inaugural lecture as Professor of

    Poetry   1858   5 *a*   3   8

  poetry   1849   42 *b*   6   22 seq.

    Quillinan on   1851   8   5   19 seq.

    W. Wordsworth [grandson] on 1858   5 *a*   3   8 seq.

  and E. Quillinan   1850   1 *b*–2 *a* 7   9

                     1850   1 *b*–2 *a* 8   3

  Crabb Robinson on   1850   39 *a*   2   10

  and Wordsworth   1851   8   5   19 seq.

  and Wordsworth's memorial   1850   37

  other references   1848   5 *b*   1   17

               [in 1847 vol.]

                     1849   77   4   10

  WORKS:

   Essays in Criticism   1865   23 *b*   3   12

   Strayed Reveller   1849   22 *b*   4   12

   [*Wordsworth's Grave*]   1851   8   5   19

ARNOLD, Thomas, D.D.

  Fragment on the Church   1844   103 *a*   4   5

                     1844   106 *b*   2   10

                     1845   1   2   3

                     1845   4   3   7

                    N.D.   2 IV K   4   9

  History of Rome   1839   2 XI 6   2   18

  Life. See Stanley, A. P.

  LETTERS:

   to Crabb Robinson   1836 100; 134

                     1837 8; 23–24

                     1839   119

   from Crabb Robinson   1837   17

ATKINSON, Henry George

  and H. Martineau   1846   92   8   13

              [in 1864 vol.]

  See also her *Letters on the Laws*

    of Man's Social Nature and

    Development

III—D

BYRON, George Gordon, Lord—*contd.*

and Lady Byron	1842	191 *b*–192 *a*	6	19
	1843	9 *b*–10 *a*	4	last
	1843	22	6	1 seq.
and Calvinism	1855	14 *a*		
and Coleridge's lectures	1849	84 *b*	7	4
and criticism	1842	125 *b*	1	15
death	1834	49	1	4
	1834	69	3	2
	1840	35	1	
epigram, by Lamb	1825	133–134	8	P.S. upside down
and Goethe	1823	95	3	3
	1829	151	1	last seq.
	1829	152	3	34 seq.
	1829	152	2	P.S.
	1829	154	1	17
and Kennedy's *Conversations on Religion*	1855	14 *a*	1	3
and Knebel	1827	12	6	last
	1828	51	2	5
and W. S. Landor	1830	60	4	1
	1836	172	1	11 seq.
	1843	25	2	7
lecture by Cooper	1847	29 *b*	5	25
Life. See Moore, T.				
and H. Martineau	1841	2	6	16
on T. Moore	1853	58 *a*	2	3
on religion. *See also* Kennedy	1821	8 19 11	1, 2	
Crabb Robinson on	1833	115	3	16 seq.
	1836	168	1	29 seq.
	1836	172	1	11 seq.
	1836	174	1	2 seq.
and Rogers. See *Question and Answer*				
and Southey	1836	168	1	29 seq.
and Southey's poems	1836	172	1	14
Tieck on	1829	154	2	5
and Wordsworth	1817	142	4	12
	1833	117	4	8
	1836	168	1	29 seq.
	1836	172	1	12 seq.
	1850	54 *b*–55 *a*	7	14
	1851	37	4	3
	1853	18	4	17
Wordsworth on	1833	117	4	8
other references	1816	135	2	10
	1828	47	4	3
	1829	94	2	5
	1832	49	2	8
	1844	80 *b*	1	22
	1851	37	4	3
	1851	37	5	2
	1859	29–30 *a*	8	19
	1866	39 *a*	4	9

[1] Miscellaneous Bundle 6 x consists of letters on this subject by various writers; as the letters are unnumbered, and are devoted entirely to the one subject, they are not included in the LETTER lists of this index.

COLERIDGE, Samuel Taylor—*contd.*

and his family	1839	103	1	21
	1849	9 b–10	5	23 seq.
and Fichte's works	1811	85 b	1	11
	1813	100 b	2	8
Barron Field on	1845	18	2	4
financial affairs	1817	145	3	1
	1831	135	3	28
and Frend	1835	120	1	16 seq.
and Hookham Frere	1817	140	1	19
	1817	141	1	13
visits Germany [1828]	1828	74		
	1850	85	1	7

[in 1849 vol.]

	1852	7	3	14
and Godwin's *Caleb Williams*	1852	10 a	3	1
and Goethe	1816	133 b	2	15
	1812	85 b	1	5
and *Faust*	1829	94	2	7
	1834	62	3	19
grave in Highgate Cemetery	1843	56–57	4	P.S.
	1851	34	2	5
and J. H. Green	1817	141	1	12
	1848	57 b	4	10 seq.
imitated by [Hancox]	1838	5 IX 13		
and Hazlitt	1816	133 a	2	last
	1845	86 a	2	18 seq.

[in 1849 vol.]

	1849	9 b–10 a	5	15
health	1808	122	1	7
	1811	60		
	1811	62	1	3
	1830	2	3	3
	1830	14	3	37
	1831	154	1	25
	1832	36	3	22
	1833	89	2	12
	1833	91	2	12
	1833	151	2	23
	1834	34	4	2
and hexameters	1840	145	2	8 seq.
	1840	146	2	20
at Highgate	1830	14	3	37
and Jacobi's works	1811	85 b	1	11
Jeux d'Esprit, by Southey [?]	1866	77 b		
and Johnson	1830	83	2	38
and Kant	1802	3 A 23	3	4
	1802	42	4	15
	1802	51	2	22
	1820	101	2	

[placed as 1814]

	N.D.	1 II 35		
and Klopstock	1810	17		P.S.
	1817	141	2	17
and C. Lamb	1811	58	4	8

COLERIDGE, Sara, Mrs. H. N.—*contd.*

and Landor's works	N.D.	21 *c*	I	4
marriage	1829	158	3	39
	1830	14	3	41
	1833	151	2	27
and her husband's illness	1842	206 *b*	4	10
	1843	5 *b*	3	last
and her husband's death	1843	9 *a*	I	8
on Mozeley's review of Arnold's *Life*	1844	122		
at Playford	1822	86–87	5	P.S.
and Mrs. Plummer	1867	83 *a–b*		
portrait by Lawrence	1852	11	2	10
	1852	12	6	10
and Quillinan	1843	125	I	3
	1846	40 *a*	2	6
	1850	11	8	6
	1850	64	4	19
on religion and church matters	1849	9 *b*–11	6	8 seq.
	1849	21 *b*	4	12 seq.
	N.D.	21 *c*	4	2 seq.
	N.D.	21 *c*		P.S.
and Crabb Robinson	1841	69 *b*	2	12
	1843	77 *b*	4	8
	1843	112 *a*	2	20
	1844	5 XVI *d*	2	13
	1846	28	I, 2	P.S. at top
	1847	9 *b*–10 *a*	7	I
	1848	24	2	8
Crabb Robinson on	1843	77 *b*	4	14
	1843	119 *a*	5	18
	1843	119 *b*–120 *b*	5	3
	1843	129 *c*	3	10
	1848	29 *a*	2	5
	1849	1 *a*–1 *b*	6	2
and the Southeys	1841	26	I	11
	1841	31		
	1841	55 *c*	3	4
	1843	33	4	11
	1843	56–57		
	1851	27	2	I
and Dora Wordsworth	1824	106	2	20
	1840	140	2	6
	1845	111 *b*–112 *a*	I	8
	1846	40 *a*	2	3
and the Wordsworths	1829	118	3	11
	1843	85	3	7
	1843	85	4	18
	1847	10 *b*–11 *a*	7	P.S.
	1848	5 *b*–6 *a*	5	7
	[in 1847 vol.]			
	1849	43 *a*	4	9
	1850	11	8	6
on the Wordsworths	1847	17 *b*	3	9 seq.
	[in 1848 vol.]			

Lamb, Charles—*contd.*
  Letters—*contd.*

to Crabb Robinson	1820	44; 47	
	1824	118	
	1825	121	
	1827	8 48 1; 6; 7 *a*; 25 *b*; 29	
	1828	44 *a*	
	1829	95 *b*; 103; 111 *a–b*	
to T. Robinson	1822	84	
to Talfourd	1828	75 *a*	
to Wordsworth	1807	81 ; N.D. [in 1810 vol.]	
		37 *a*	

Lamb, Mary Ann. *See also* Lamb,
  Charles and Mary

and her brother's death	1834	79	2	2
	1835	143	13	10
arrangements for, after her brother's death	1834	79	3	4
	1835	93		
	1836	181	2	27
	1839	73	1	6 seq.
	1842	132 *a*	2	4
	1844	7 *a*	5	10
and her brother's work at the East India House	1835	146	2	11
	1835	148	3	9
and Sara Coleridge	1841	71 *b*	3	19
	1841	85 *a*	4	17
and Coleridge	1811	38	4	1
	1813	90	1	3
death	1847	26 *b*	3	5
funeral	1847	27	6	9
	1847	28 *b*	2	P.S.
health	1809	16	2	19
	1810	32	2	17
	1810	35	1	14
	1810	35	3	12
	N.D.	37 *a*	1	4
[in 1810 vol.]				
	1811	38	4	1
	1815	125	3	6
	1816	135	3	13
	1821	69	2	9
	1821	70	1	5
	1822	75	3	13
	1822	86–87	4	last
	1823	66–68	11	5
endorsed 1821				
	1825	120	1	P.S.
	1825	125–126	2	8
	1825	125–126	5	19
	1825	133–134	7	17
	1825	135	1	19
	1825	136	1	20
	1826	150	3	11

---

[1] Owing to the difficulty of the handwriting, Capel Lofft's letters are very imperfectly indexed.

[1] Cf. *Correspondence of Henry Crabb Robinson with the Wordsworth Circle*, p. 100, note 1.

[ROBINSON, Mary]
    Vancenza; or the Dangers of Credulity 1792   40   2   15
ROBINSON, Robert. *Life.* *See* Dyer, G.
ROGERS, Samuel

and his bank's notes	1846	46	4	8
	1846	47	4	3
	1846	164 *b*	3	4
[in 1840 vol.]				
and the bank robbery	1844	107 *a*	1	4
	1844	107 *b*–108 *a*	2	9
	1844	107 *b*–108 *a*	6	2
Behne's medallion	1856	42 *a*	1	3
breakfast parties	1845	67 *a*	2	18
	1846	13	3	17
	1846	16 *b*–17 *a*	5	4
	1846	19 *b*–20	7	4
	1846	23 *a*	4	8
	1846	24	2	8
	1848	29 *a*	2	11
	1851	9	6	6
	1851	16 *b*–17 *a*	5	last
	1851	32	8	12
	1853	26	3	5
Byron's verses (*Question and Answer*)	1833	115	3	17
annoyed by beggars, and Doyle's				
caricature [1]	1842	196 *b*	3	12 seq.
	1842	199	2	1 seq.
	1842	200 *b*	3	15
death and funeral	1855	89 *a*		
	1855	89 *b*		
dinner party	1845	15	2	15
	1847	1 *b*–2 *b*	2	11 seq.
and J. W. Donaldson	1847	1 *b*–2 *b*	2	9
	1847	1 *b*–2 *b*	5	1
	1848	68 *b*	4	1
and the Flaxman Gallery	1847	29 *b*	6	3
	1847	43 *b*	2	12 seq.
	1847	45	2	19
	1847	48 *b*	3	17
	1848	31 *a*	4	7
[in 1847 vol.]				
	1848	26 *b*	5	2
	1849	2 IV xiii	6	4
	1853	64–65	6	5
and Gervinus	1846	16 *b*–17 *a*	5	4
health	1844	9 *b*–10 *a*	7	14
	1845	111 *b*–112 *a*	7	2
	1849	35 *b*	4	1
	1850	53 *b*	3	2
	1850	63	4	19
	1851	60 *b*	2	16
	1851	76 *b*–77 *a*	2	13
	1853	26	3	5

[1] Cf. H. C. R. Diary, 5th Nov. 1842, and *Correspondence of Henry Crabb Robinson with the Wordsworth Circle*, p. 470, note 1.

III—K

WYNN, The Rt. Hon. Charles Watkyn
     Williams—*contd.*

and the Southey Family	1841	26	I	6
	1841	35	I	4
	1841	45 *c*	I	6
	1841	64 *a*	I	6
	1848	29 *b*	2	9

YORKE, Philip, 2nd Earl of Hardwick
     Athenian Letters   1801   3 A 9   2   15

II. TITLES

Published works to which reference under the author may be found.

Charity Ball, The. Byron, Lord.
Chartism. Carlyle, T.
Childe Harold's Pilgrimage. Byron, Lord.
Christabel. Coleridge, S. T.
Christian Aspects of Faith and Duty. Tayler, J. J.
Church of Christ not an Ecclesiasticism. James, Henry.
Cid, The, appendix. Southey, R.
Citation and Examination of William Shakespeare. Landor, W. S.
Clubs of London. Marsh, C.
Colombe's Birthday. Browning, R.
Commentaries. Blackstone, Sir W.
Commonplace Book. Southey, R.
Comparison of the Institutions of Moses with those of the Hindoos, etc.
 Priestley, J.
Complete Guide to the English Lakes. Martineau, H.
Confessional. Blackburne, F.
Confessions of an English Opium Eater. De Quincey, T.
—— *of an Inquiring Spirit.* Coleridge, S. T.
Conquest of Scinde. Napier, Sir William.
Constitutional History of England. Hallam, H.
Country Neighbours. Burney, S. H.
Crofton Boys. Playfellow, The. Martineau, H.
Curiosities of Literature. Disraeli, I.
Curse of Kehama. Southey, R.

Dark Ages. Maitland, S. R.
David Copperfield. Dickens, C.
Devotional Taste. Barbauld, A. L.
Diary in France. Wordsworth, C.
Diary Illustrative of the Times of George II. Bury, Lady C.
Diogenes' Lanthorn. Taylor, T.
Discourse on Matters Pertaining to Religion. Parker, T.
Discourse on the Study of the Law of Nature and Nations.
 Mackintosh, Sir J.
Disquisitions, Metaphysical and Literary. Sayers, F.
Diversions of Purley. ΈΠΕΑ ΠΤΕΡΟ'ΕΝΤΑ. Tooke, J. H.
Divine Drama of History and Civilization. Smith, James.
Doctor, The. Southey, R.
Doctrine of Original Sin Defended. Edwards, J.
Don Juan. Byron, Lord.
Dred. Stowe, H. E. B.

Early Recollections chiefly relating to the late S. T. Coleridge. Cottle, J.
Eastern Life, Past and Present. Martineau, H.
Edmund Oliver. Lloyd, C.
Edwin the Fair. Taylor, Sir H.
Elements of the Human Mind. Stewart, Dugald.
Elements of the Philosophy of the Mind. Belsham, T.
Ellen Middleton. Fullerton, Lady.
Eloquence of the British Senate. Hazlitt, W.
Emmeline, or the Orphan of the Castle. Smith, C.
End of Religious Controversy. Milner, J.
Enquirer. Godwin, W.
Enquiry concerning Political Justice. Godwin, W.

Enquiry into our Ideas of the Sublime and Beautiful. Burke, E.
—— *into the State of the Nation at the Commencement of the Present Administration.* Pamphlet. Brougham, H. P.
Eōthen. Kinglake, A. W.
Ernest. Lofft, C.
Errors of Romanism. Whately, R.
Esmond. Thackeray, W. M.
Essay on the Development of Christian Doctrine. Newman, J. H.
—— *on the Freedom of the Will.* Edwards, J.
—— *on the Impolicy of the African Slave Trade.* Clarkson, T.
—— *on Italian Literature.* Hobhouse, Sir J. C.
—— *on Literary Character.* Disraeli, I.
—— *on the Nature and Principles of Taste.* Alison, A.
—— *on the Principles of Human Action.* Hazlitt, W.
—— *on the Principle of Population.* Malthus, T. R.
—— *on the Rate of Wages.* Carey, H. C.
—— *on the Slavery and Commerce of the Human Species,* Clarkson, T.
Essays. Emerson, R. W.
——. Whately, R.
—— *in Criticism.* Arnold, M.
—— *in Ecclesiastical Biography.* Stephen, Sir J.
—— *of Elia.* Lamb, C.
—— *on the Formation and Publication of Opinions and other Subjects.* Bailey, S.
—— *in a Series of Letters to a Friend.* Foster, J.
Essential Principles of the Wealth of Nations. Pamphlet. Gray, J.
Essentials of English History. Littlewood, W. E.
Eugene Aram. Lytton, Lord.
Eve of the Conquest and Other Poems. Taylor, H.
Evelina. D'Arblay, F.
Examination of a Sermon preached at Cambridge by Robert Hall on Modern Infidelity. Robinson, A.
Excursion, The. Wordsworth, W.

Fare thee Well. Byron, Lord.
Farmer's Boy, The. Bloomfield, R.
Feats on the Fjord. Playfellow, The. Martineau, H.
Female Biography. Hays, M.
Fleetwood. Godwin, W.
Forest and Game Law Tales. Martineau, H.
Fossils of the South Downs. Mantell, G. A.
Fragment on the Church. Arnold, T.
Frankenstein. Shelley, M. W.
Friend, The. Coleridge, S. T.

Gebir. Landor, W. S.
Genealogies of our Lord and Saviour Jesus Christ. Hervey, A.
General Biographical Dictionary, The. Chalmers, A.
Geraldine. Agnew, E. C.
Geraldine Fauconberg. Burney, S. H.
Geraldine: a Sequel to Christabel. Tupper, M. F.
German Anti-supernaturalism. Harwood, P.
German and English Dictionary. Crabb, G.
German Grammar. Crabb, G.

German Romance. Carlyle, T.
Germany from 1760 to 1814. Austin, S.
Glencoe. Talfourd, Sir T. N.
God in Christ. Bevan.
Great Opportunities. Stanley, A. P.
Gresford Vale and Other Poems. Holford, M.
Grongar Hill. Dyer, J.

Hear Both Sides. Holcroft, T.
Heaven and Earth. Byron, Lord.
Helen. Edgeworth, M.
Herald of Sight. Harris, T. L.
Herman and Dorothea. Holcroft, T.
——. tr. Whewell, W.
High and Low Life in Italy. Landor, W. S.
Hints towards a formation of a more Comprehensive Theory of Life.
    Coleridge, S. T.
Historic Survey of German Poetry. Taylor, W.
Historical Dialogues for Young People. Hays, M.
History of Egypt. Sharpe, S.
—— *of England.* Froude, J. A.
—— ——. Lingard, J.
—— ——. Macaulay, T. B.
—— ——. Mackintosh, Sir J.
—— —— *during the Thirty Years' Peace.* Martineau, H.
—— *of English Dramatic Poetry.* Collier, J. P.
—— *of Europe.* Alison, Sir A.
—— *of Great Britain.* Henry, R.
—— *of Greece.* Thirlwall, C.
—— *of Hallamshire.* Hunter, J.
—— *of Kent.* Hasted, E.
—— *of Latin Christianity, The.* Milman, H. H.
—— *of Rome.* Arnold, T.
—— *of Scotland.* Laing, M.
—— *of Spanish Literature.* Ticknor, G.
—— *of the Abolition of the Slave Trade.* Clarkson, T.
—— *of the British Colonies in the West Indies.* Edwards, B.
—— *of the French Revolution.* Carlyle, T.
—— *of the Hebrew Monarchy.* Newman, F. W.
—— *of the Peninsular War.* Southey, R.
—— *of the Popes.* Austin, W.
—— *of the Speculative Society of Edinburgh.* Ferguson, W.
—— *of the University and Colleges of Cambridge.* Dyer, G.
—— *of Wales.* Warrington, William.
Honington Green. A ballad. Bloomfield, N.
Hour and the Man. Martineau, H.
Household Education. Martineau, H.
Human Body and its Connection with Man. Wilkinson, J. J. G.

Idylls of the King. Tennyson, A.
Illustrations of Northern Antiquities. Weber, H. W.
—— *of Political Economy.* Martineau, H.
Imaginary Conversations. Landor, W. S.

Improvisations from the Spirit. Wilkinson, J. J. G.
Independent Man. Ensor, G.
Ingoldsby Legends. Barham, R. H.
Inheritance. Ferrier, S. E.
In Memoriam. Tennyson, A.
Inquiry into the nature and character of the Possessive Augment. Manning, J.
Introduction to Entomology. Spence, A. W.
Introduction to the Study of the Greek Classic Poets. Coleridge, H. N.
Ion. Talfourd, Sir T. N.
Iphigenia in Tauris. tr. Taylor, W.
Isle of the Sirens. Whewell, W.
Italian. Radcliffe, A. W.
Italian Sonnets. tr. Glassford, J.
Italy. Rogers, S.
Italy Past and Present. Gallenga, A. C. N.

Jack Sheppard. Ainsworth, W. H.
Jane Eyre. Brontë, C.
Joan of Arc. Southey, R.
Job. Blake, W.
Journal in France in 1845. Travels in France. Allies, T. W.
Journal of a Residence in Norway. Laing, S.
Journey throughout Ireland in 1834. Inglis, H. D.
Juridical Essays. Randall, E.
Justice of the Peace. Burn, R.

Lalla Rookh. Moore, T.
Land We Live In. Knight, C.
Last Days of Pompeii. Lytton, Lord.
Latter Day Pamphlets. Carlyle, T.
Lay of the Last Minstrel. Scott, Sir W.
Lazarus and Other Poems. Plumptre, E. H.
Lectures on the Dramatic Literature of the Reign of Queen Elizabeth. Hazlitt, W.
—— *on the History of France.* Stephen, J.
Letter concerning the Two First Chapters of Luke. Taylor, W.
—— *to a Noble Lord.* Burke, E.
—— *to the Duke of Portland.* Burke, E.
—— *to the Rt. Hon. H. Dundas with the sketch of a Negro Code.* Burke, E.
—— *to William Smith, Esq. J.P.* Southey, R.
Letters from Canada. Traill, C. P.
—— *from England by Don Manuel A. Espriella.* Southey, R.
—— *from Italy to a Younger Sister.* Taylor, C.
—— *from the Mountains.* Grant, A.
—— *on Chivalry and Romance.* Hurd, R.
—— *on Mesmerism.* Martineau, H.
—— *on the Laws of Man's Social Nature and Development.* Martineau, H.
—— *on the Poor Law in Ireland.* De Vere, A. T.
—— *to his Son.* Chesterfield, Lord.
Life of Addison. Aikin, L.
—— *of Lorenzo de Medici.* Roscoe, W.
—— *of Napoleon Buonaparte.* Scott, Sir W.
—— *Public and Private, of Lord Eldon.* Twiss, H.
—— *in the Sick-room.* Martineau, H.

Passages from the Diary of a Late Physician. Warren, S.
Past and Present. Carlyle, T.
Pelham. Lytton, Lord.
Pericles and Aspasia. Landor, W. S.
Peveril of the Peak. Scott, Sir W.
Phantasmagoria, or Sketches of Life and Character. Jewsbury, M. J.
Phases of Faith. Newman, F. W.
Philip van Artevelde. Taylor, Sir H.
Philosophy of Comte. Martineau, H.
Physical Theory of Another Life. Taylor, Isaac.
Pictorial History of England. Craik, G. L.
Playfellow, The. Martineau, H.
Poetical Sketches. Blake, W.
Poet's Fate. Dyer, G.
Political Index to the Histories of Great Britain and Ireland. Beatson, R.
Poor Laws and Paupers Illustrated. Martineau, H.
Popular Ballads. Jamieson, R.
Portraiture of Quakerism. Clarkson, T.
Practical Christianity. More, H.
Practical Education. Edgeworth, M.
Prelude, The. Wordsworth, W.
Princess, The. Morgan, Lady.
Proofs of a Conspiracy. Robinson, J.
Proverbial Philosophy. Tupper, M. F.
Pursuits of Literature. Mathias, T. J.

Redgauntlet. Scott, Sir W.
Reflections on the French Revolution. Burke, E.
Relation between Judaism and Christianity. Palfrey, J. G.
Religion of the Nineteenth Century. Stanley, A. P.
Remarks on Mr. J. P. Collier's and Mr. C. Knight's editions of Shakespeare.
    Dyce, A.
Remorse. Coleridge, S. T.
Representative Men. Emerson, R. W.
Retrospect of the Religious Life of England. Tayler, J. J.
Retrospect of Western Travel. Martineau, H.
Reynard the Fox. Naylor, S.
Rhetoric. Blair, Hugh.
Rioters. Martineau, H.
Road to Ruin. Holcroft, T.
Rokeby. Scott, Sir W.
Romance of the Forest. Radcliffe, A. W.
Romance of Private Life. Burney, S. H.
Rome in the Nineteenth Century. Eaton, C. A.
Rural and Domestic Life of Germany. Howitt, W.
Rural Tales. Bloomfield, R.
Ruth. Gaskell, E. C. S.

Sabbation; Honor Neale and Other Poems. Trench, R. C.
St. Leon. Godwin, W.
Sakuntala, or the Fatal Ring. Jones, Sir W.
Sardanapalus. Byron, Lord.
Satire upon Satirists. Landor, W. S.
Saturday Evening. Taylor, Isaac.
Series of Adventures in the Course of a Voyage up the Red Sea. Irwin, E.

Sermons. Blair, Hugh.
——. Robertson, F. W.
—— *before the University of Oxford.* Newman, J. H.
Settlers at Home. Playfellow, The. Martineau, H.
Sights and Thoughts in Foreign Churches. Faber, F. W.
Silas Marner. Evans, M. A. (George Eliot).
Sinai and Palestine. Stanley, A. P.
Society in America. Martineau, H.
Son of the Soil. Oliphant, M. O.
Soul: Her Sorrows and her Aspirations. Newman, F. W.
Spirit of the East. Urquhart, D.
Springtime with the Poets. Martin, F.
State in its Relations with the Church. Gladstone, W. E.
Suffolk Bartholomeans: A memoir of John Meadows. Taylor, Edgar.
Sybil. Disraeli, B.

Table Talk. Coleridge, S. T.
Tales. Edgeworth, M.
Tales from Shakespeare. Lamb, C.
Temple of Nature. Darwin, E.
Thaddeus of Warsaw. Porter, J.
Thalaba. Southey, R.
Theodore Cyphon. Walker, G.
Theodore or the Enthusiast. Hare-Naylor, F.
Theological Essays. Maurice, J. F. D.
Thoughts on Man. Godwin, W.
Travels in France. Holcroft, T.
Travels in Turkey. De Vere, A. T.
Travels of an Irish Gentleman in search of a Religion. Moore, T.
Travels to Discover the Source of the Nile. Bruce, J.
Treasure or Storehouse of Similies. Cawdry, R.
Treatise on Prison Discipline. Field, J.
Tremaine. Ward, R. P.
Trials of Margaret Lindsay. Wilson, J.
Triumphs of Temper. Hayley, W.
True Intellectual System of the Universe. Cudworth, R.
Tour through Italy. Eustace, J. C.
Tour in Wales. Pennant, T.
Two Hundred Years Ago. Mountfield, D.
Two Old Men's Tales. Marsh, A. C.

Uncle Tom's Cabin. Stowe, H. E. B.
Unspoken Sermons. MacDonald, G.

Vacation Rambles and Thoughts. Talfourd, Sir T. N.
Vancenza; or the Dangers of Credulity. Robinson, M.
Vanity Fair. Thackeray, W. M.
Vaurien or Sketches of the Times. Disraeli, I.
Vestiges of the Natural History of Creation. Chambers, R.
Vicar of Wakefield. Taylor, T.
View of the Evidences of Christianity. Paley, W.
View of the Scripture Revelations concerning a Future State. Whately, W.
View of Society and Manners in France. Moore, J.
Villette. Brontë, C.
Vision of Judgment. Southey, R.

Walk through Wales.   Warner, R.
Wallenstein.   Tr. Coleridge, S. T.
Wanderings of Warwick.   Smith, C.
War, Cholera, and the Ministry of Health.   Wilkinson, J. J. G.
Way to Keep Him.   Murphy, A.
Werner.   Byron, Lord.
Within and Without.   MacDonald, G.
Wives and Daughters.   Gaskell, E. C. S.
Woman's Mission.   Lewis.
Words of Christ.   Field, C.
Worthies of Yorkshire and Lancashire.   Coleridge, Hartley.

Youth and Age.   Coleridge, S. T.

Zincali; or an Account of the Gypsies in Spain.   Borrow, G.

GENERAL INDEX

GENERAL INDEX

Since the whole book consists of Crabb Robinson's opinions and criticisms on *Books and Their Writers*, these are not separately indexed under his name. His criticisms of a book he is reading so often lead him from the subject of the book itself to comment on the character of the author, that his more important personal opinions may generally be found among the references to an author's works.

The following signs should be noted:

[ ] indicate information supplied by the editor.

⟨ ⟩ indicate a paraphrase in the text, e.g. '⟨*Biographia Literaria*⟩' appears on p. 182 as 'two volumes of Miscellanies,' on pp. 200 and 210 as Coleridge's 'Memoirs,' and on p. 213 as 'Coleridge's book.'

‖ indicates a typographical, spelling or other error in the text, e.g. '‖ Lawrence, James Henry, poem,' in the index indicates a correction of 'Laurence, *The Knight of Malta*,' p. 646; '‖ Parken, 55, 85, 87, 88' in the index indicates that 'Parker,' p. 55, and 'Parkin,' p. 85, should read 'Parken' throughout.

⟨ABBOTSFORD⟩, 266
ABEILLA, 11
ABERDEEN, visited, 433
ABINGER, 1st baron. *See* Scarlett, James
ABINGTON, Frances, 55
ABLETT, Joseph, 495
ABOLITION. *See* Slavery
ADAIR, J. M., 352
ADAMS, Dr. Joseph, 36, 48
ADAMS, Mrs., 36
ADDISON, Joseph
    lecture by Hazlitt, 226
    mentioned by Thackeray, 721, 725
  WORK:
    Cato acted, 26
ADERS, Charles, 56, 58, 106, 119, 122, 307, 310, 392, 442
ADERS, Eliza [Mrs. Charles]
    on Byron's ⟨*Question and Answer*⟩, 422
    Carlyle and, 825, 828
    and Coleridge, 361, 405, 442
    gifts to Crabb Robinson, 511, 625; letter to Crabb Robinson, 687
    described by Rogers, 422
    and Wordsworth, 361; portrait of Wordsworth, 618
  mentioned, 281, 331, 345, 406, 426

BLAKE, William—*contd.*
　article by Crabb Robinson, 15, 31
　death, 353
　Life. See Cunningham, A., *Lives of the Most Eminent British
　　Painters*
　　Gilchrist, A., *Life of Blake*
　state of his mind, 40, 41, 355, 498, 752

　writings and works of art:
　　exhibition, 15; sale, 705
　　'Canterbury Pilgrims,' 325, 353, 356
　　Catalogue, 15, 625, 717
　　Chimney Sweeper, 25
　　Jerusalem, 41
　　Job, 331
　　Poems, 85, 117, 625, 717
　　Prose, 810
　　Songs of Innocence, 669
　　(*Songs of Innocence and Experience*), ed. Wilkinson, 675, 676
　　songs, 810
　　illustrations for Young's (*Night Thoughts*), 25, 117
　mentioned, 20, 361, 550, 706, 799
BLAKESLEY, Joseph Williams, 509
BLANC, Louis, 783
BLESSINGTON, Charles John Gardiner, Earl of, 411
BLESSINGTON, Marguerite, Countess of
　principal entries, 411 seq., 420, 421, 423 seq., 438, 440, 443, 450, 451,
　　456, 458, 460, 464, 465, 468, 488, 489, 492, 506, 511, 549, 551,
　　572
　her Book of Beauty, 438, 750
　and Count D'Orsay, 469
　financial position, 426, 469, 689
　leaving for France, 689
　in D. Quillinan's letter, 509
　and Crabb Robinson, 456, 491, 549, 749
　and N. P. Willis, 443, 445, 450, 460, 464
　mentioned, 383, 491, 497, 504, 561, 575, 631, 746

　WORKS:
　　writings, 426, 689
　　(*Conversations with Lord Byron*), 411, 412, 415, 457
　　Memoirs [ed. Madden, R. R.], 749, 750
　　Repealer, The, 426
　　Two Friends, The, 456

BLEWITT, Octavian, 759
BLOMEFIELD, Francis (*Essay towards a Topographical History of the
　　County of Norfolk*), 645
(BLOMFIELD, Charles James), Bishop of London, 664, 697, 698, 732
BLOOMFIELD, Robert, 28, 202, 394, 409
BLOSSETT, Serjeant, 225
BOADEN, James
　Life of Mrs. Inchbald, 456
　Life of Mrs. Siddons, 354
BOCCACCIO, 407
BODICHON, Mme, note 680
BOEHMEN, Jacob, 88, 108, 327

III—M

COLERIDGE, Samuel Taylor—*contd.*
　WORKS—*contd.*
　　Osorio. See *Remorse*
　　(*Rash Conjuror*), 108
　　Remorse, 23, 112, 116, 119, 652, 664
　　—— first performance, 117, 843
　　—— profit on, 118, 128
　　—— review, 146
　　(*Seven Lectures on Shakespeare and Milton*), ed. Collier, J. P., 761, 763, 839
　　(*Sibylline Leaves*), 182
　　Sonnet to Lord Stanhope, 501, 503
　　Statesman's Manual. See *Lay Sermon*
　　Table Talk, ed. Coleridge, H. N., 464, 465, 506, 586
　　—— review, 462
　　We are Seven, 481
　　(*Zapolya*), 182
COLERIDGE, Sara, Mrs. H. N.
　　introduction to Dr. Brabant, 663 and note
　　and Hartley Coleridge, 686
　　and S. T. Coleridge, 669, 680, 681, 697
　　editing S. T. Coleridge's works, 636, 659, 661 seq., 687 seq., 691, 701
　　and J. Cottle, 680, 681
　　death, 716
　　personal qualities:
　　　as a child, 190
　　　as a girl, 270, 271
　　gift from Crabb Robinson, 665
　　on Crabb Robinson's *Supplement* to Clarkson's *Strictures*, 568
　　and Southey's niece, 693, 694
　　and Wordsworth, 661, 662, 681, 697
　　on the Wordsworths, 709 and note
　　marginalia in Wordsworth's *Life*, 803
　　mentioned, 570, 581, 592
　　WORKS:
　　　translation (M. Dobrizhopfer, *Account of the Abipones*), 270
　　　Phantasmion, 538
COLERIDGE, Sara, Mrs. S. T., *born* Fricker, 27, 189, 271, 297
COLERIDGE, William Hart [Bishop], 446 and note, 488
COLERIDGE FAMILY, 446 and note, 488, 501, 502, 685
COLISEUM, visited with Wordsworth, 520
COLLIER, Jane, 16, 26, 55, 87, 145, 163, 218
COLLIER, John Dyer, 3, 16, 145
COLLIER, John Payne
　　articles on: *Athenæum*, 795; *Saturday Review*, 797
　　and the Camden Society, 548
　　and Coleridge's lectures, 52. *See also* Coleridge, S. T., *Seven Lectures upon Shakespeare and Milton*, ed. Collier, J. P.
　　and the Duke of Devonshire, 403
　　accused of forgery. *See* his ed. of Shakespeare
　　and Gifford's notes on Shirley, 344

GERMAN
  editions:
  —— *British Poets*, 366
  —— Byron's works, 369, 370
  —— translations from Coleridge and Wordsworth, 366, 531
  literature, 353, 367, 773
  —— article by: Carlyle, 580; Macaulay, 353
  —— Crabb Robinson and, 4, 25 seq., 33, 146, 245, 374, 426, 546, 634;
      advice to Carlyle, 319, 335, 823 seq.; translation from. *See*
      Robinson, H. C., works
  philosophy, 70, 191, 307
  See also under particular philosophers and individual opinions
German Playwrights, article by Carlyle, 580
GERMANY
  Coleridge's letters from, 466
  article on *Prussian Reform*, 299, 318 and note, seq.
  —— Religion in, 552
  visited, 224, 366 seq., 446 seq.
  —— with Wordsworth, 528 seq.
GERVINUS, G. G., 658
GIBBON, Edward, 759, 774
  (*History of the Decline and Fall of the Roman Empire*, abridged edn.,
    1789), 496
GIBBS, Michael, 745
(GIBBS, Sir Vicary), Attorney-General, 77
GIBSON, John, 395
GIBSON, Dr., 740, 794
GIBSON, 692
GIFFORD, William, 63, 225, 311, 344
  notes on Shirley, 344
GILBERT, Miss, 60
GILBERTS, The, 23
GILCHRIST, Alexander, 752, 799
  Life of Blake, 809 seq.
  —— review, 810
GILCHRIST, James, 322 and note, seq.
GILES, essay on E. Elliott, 710
GILLIES, Margaret
  portrait of: M. Wordsworth, 582, 660, 781; W. Wordsworth, 582, 781
GILLMAN, James
  and Coleridge, 185, 200, 506
  and Cottle's letters from Coleridge, 499, 501 seq.
  mentioned, 208, 293, 320, 488
  WORK:
  Life of S. T. Coleridge, 549
GILLMAN, Mrs., 293, 687
GIORDANO, Lucca
  pictures, 711
  sonnet by Wordsworth, 711
GIOTTO, 524
GLADSTONE, William Ewart, 564 seq.
  WORKS:
  (*State in its Relations with the Church*), 563 seq.
  —— review, 569

GODWIN, William—*contd.*
WORKS:
writings, 1, 274; influence on the drama, 377; proposed German edition, 206, 208 seq.
Caleb Williams, 2, 215, 345
Deloraine, 423
Enquiry concerning Political Justice, 3, 6, 25, 27, 199, 841
Faulkner, 118
History of the Commonwealth, 338
Life of Geoffrey Chaucer, review, 28
Mandeville, 212, 215, 216. *See also* writings, proposed German edn.
Of Population, in Answer to Mr. Malthus, 263 seq., 587
Pamphlet, 221
St. Leon, 7
Thoughts on Man, 418 seq.
GODWIN, William [son], 241, 299, 307, 316, 317
GODWINIAN notion, a, 806
GODWINS, The, 142, 152, 155, 162 seq., 167, 263, 275, 299, 574
GOESCHEL, Karl Friedrich (*Unterhaltungen zur Schilderung Goetheischer Dicht- und Denkweise*), 495
GOETHE, August von, 751
GOETHE, Johann Wolfgang von
main entry, 367 seq.
on Byron and his works, 224, 339, 438, 450, 746. *See also* Robinson, H. C., letter to Moore
supposed death, 400
death, 405
Lewes inquires concerning, 751 seq.
literary obligations, 776
portrait, 491
on Sir W. Scott, 438
on Vico, 321
other references, 89, 114, 308, 402, 403, 425, 478, 480, 507, 562, 619, 627 seq., 651, 656, 658, 789
BOOKS, ETC., RELATING TO:
Arnold, M., *Essays in Criticism*, 822
—— *Memorial Verses*, 745
Austin, S., *Characteristics of Goethe*, 430, 467; review, 426
Beddoes, T. L., *Poems, with a Memoir*, 713
Goeschel, *Unterhaltungen zur Schilderung Goetheischer Dicht- und Denkweise*
Lewes, G. H., *Life of Goethe*, 495, 756
article:
by Carlyle, 409, 581
by Crabb Robinson, *Goethe's Works*, 408, 415, 416, 426, 430, 638 and note
mentioned, 252, 286, 410, 411, 414, 467, 506, 512, 515, 540, 545, 566, 679, 690, 709, 717, 727
WORKS:
article on English Literature, 438
Braut von Corinth, 180, 628
Briefwechsel mit einem Kind. See Arnim, von
Correspondence with Knebel, 751, 759
Correspondence with Zelter, 374

—————

[1] K. A. Esdaile. Cf. *The Library*, 3rd series, vol. v.

WILBERFORCES, The, 551
    and Clarkson. *See* Clarkson and the Wilberforces
WILD, 21
WILKES, John, 23, 73, 512
    in Byron's *Vision of Judgment*, 286, 367, 370
WILKES, Mary, 23, 73
WILKINSON, James John Garth, 675 seq., 705
    Human Body, The, 761 and note
WILKINSON, Joseph (*Select Views in Cumberland, Westmorland, and Lancashire*), with an introduction by W. Wordsworth, 47, 111
WILLIAM IV, death, 529
WILLIAMS, Helen Maria, 147, 148, 150, 182, 209, 217, 224, 225, 230 seq., 248, 255, 283, 848
  WORKS:
    writings, 147, 148, 176
      verses to T. Clarkson, 152
    (*Letters on the State of Politics in France*), 230 seq.
    Narrative of the Events that have taken place in France, 176
WILLIAMS, Sir Roger, narrative in *Tracts of the Somers Family*, 174
WILLIAMS, The Rev. —, 360
WILLIS, Nathaniel Parker, 443 seq., 450, 460, 464, 488, 489, 491, 540
  WORKS:
    Hymn, 'The perfect world by Adam trod,' 445
    Pencillings by the Way, 444 and note, 445, 467
WILLMOTT, Robert Aris
  WORKS:
    Bishop Jeremy Taylor, 692
    Journal of Summertime in the Country, 692
WILSON, John, pseud. Christopher North
    and Jeffrey and Wordsworth, 151, 160, 161, 196, 256, 467, 486, 699
    other references, 188, 195, 267, 478, 635
  WORKS:
    writings, 82, 83, 130, 140
    City of the Plague, 186
    Isle of Palms and other Poems, 130, 140
      —— review, 82, 151
    Noctes Ambrosianae, 316
WILSON, Sir Robert, 438
WILSON, Walter, 357
WILSON [barrister], 398, 400
WIMBRIDGE, 574 and note
WINCKELMANN, Johann Joachim, 410
WINDHAM, William, 12, 54
WINDSOR, visited by M. Lamb, 128
WIRGMAN, Thomas, 92, 107
WISEMAN, Nicholas Patrick Stephen, Cardinal, 605
WODD, Henry, 40
WOLCOT, John, pseud. Peter Pindar, 32
WOLFE, Charles, *Memoirs*, 339
WOLLSTONECRAFT, Mary. *See* Godwin
WOOD, Dr., 597
WOOD, 112

WORDSWORTH, William—*contd.*

portrait by: Mrs. Aders, 618; T. Carrick, 674; R. Carruthers, 217; Miss Gillies, 582, 781; (Hancock), 500, 502; Haydon, 239 seq.; H. H. Pickersgill, 457 seq.; H. W. Pickersgill, 426, 715; J. Severn, 521; Slater, 509; T. Woolner, 707, 708; L. C. Wyon, 664, 665, 674; W. Wyon, 572

and Sir R. Price, 538, 539

and D. Quillinan. *See* Quillinan, Dorothy, last illness and death; Quillinan, E., marriage

breach with E. Quillinan, 671, 672, 674, 681

at Quillinan's with Mrs. Wordsworth, 357

and F. Reynolds, 460

and J. C. Richmond, 694, 695

and Rio's book, 618, 619 note

and Anthony Robinson, 74, 92, 103

and Crabb Robinson, 189, 287, 288, 438, 523, 531, 533 seq., 670, 697

Crabb Robinson an amanuensis for, 459, 460, 528, 649

dedication to Crabb Robinson, 1, 592, 603, 608 and note, 611 seq.

Crabb Robinson as an executor, 457, 495, 604

gift to Crabb Robinson, 849

gifts from Crabb Robinson, 442, 443, 591, 639, 640, 643, 651, 653

introduction to Crabb Robinson, 2 and note, 6, 10, 11, 845

Crabb Robinson's visits to Rydal: 1816, 186 and note seq., 850; 1821, 271 seq.; 1826, 339 seq.; 1833, 427 seq.; 1835, 469 seq.; 1838, 559 seq.; 1840, 587 seq.; 1841, 603 seq.; 1842, 621 seq.; 627 seq.; 1843, 637 seq.; 1844, 647 seq.; 1845, 655 seq.; 1846, 660 seq., 854; 1847, 670 seq., 854; 1848, 682 seq., 854; 1849, 693, 694

and Rogers, 488

at Rogers's, 293, 300, 458, 462, 534, 535, 570, 595

at Miss Rogers's, 493

and the Royal Society of Literature, 641 and note, 642

in Rome, 519, 520

and a Sarnen coachman, 244, 245, 249

and Schiller, 245

and Schlosser, 531

in Scotland, 1803 itinerary, 274 and note; 1833 tour, 427, 430, 433

and J. Severn, 520, 521

shipwreck, 256

at the Society of Arts, 292

and the Misses Solly, 662

and R. Southey, 40, 41, 179, 579

and Southey's *Doctor*, 563

and Southey's niece, 693

and the Southey family troubles, 590

stamp office appointment, 125, 358, 457, 486, 570, 617

statue by Thrupp, 717, 724, 731, 834 seq.

call on D. Stuart, 170

and C. Taggart's *Poems*, 443 and note

and T. N. Talfourd, 120, 121, 491, 682, 697

at Talfourd's, 295, 296, 356, 494, 496, 497, 569

TITLES

Titles and first lines to which reference under the author may be found. Biographical works and the works of Shakespeare and Milton are not included.

Abbot, The. Scott, Sir W.
Abridgment of the Light of Nature Pursued, by Abraham Tucker. Hazlitt, W.
Absentee, The. Edgeworth, M.
Adam Bede. Evans, M. A. (George Eliot)
Adela Cathcart. MacDonald, G.
Admiral's Daughter, The. Marsh, A. C.
Adonais. Shelley, P. B.
Adventures of a Younger Son. Trelawny, E. J.
—— *of Susan Hopley.* Crowe, M.
—— *of Ulysses.* Lamb, C.
Advice to His Son. Osborne, F.
After Dark. Collins, W. W.
Aids to Reflection. Coleridge, S. T.
Album Verses. Lamb, C.
Alchemist, The. Jonson, B.
Alfred. Cottle, J.
Alfred de Musset. Palgrave, F. T.
Alice. Lytton, Lord.
Alliance between Church and State. Warburton, W.
Alton Locke. Kingsley, C.
Amatonda. tr., Robinson, H. C.
American Notes for General Circulation. Dickens, C.
Anastasius. Hope, T.
Ancient Mariner, The. Coleridge, S. T.
—— *Scottish Poems.* Pinkerton, J.
'And is it among rude untutored Dales?' Wordsworth, W.
Andrea of Hungary. Landor, W. S.
Anna St. Ives. Holcroft, T.
Annals of a Quiet Neighbourhood. MacDonald, G.
—— *of the Parish.* Galt, J.
Anne of Geierstein. Scott, Sir W.
Answer to the Address of the Rt. Hon. H. Grattan to his Fellow Citizens. Duigenan, P.
Antigone. Sophocles.
Antiquary, The. Scott, Sir W.
Apologia pro Vitâ Suâ. Newman, J. H.
Appeal to the Middle Classes. Newman, F. W.
Apple, The. Crosse, A.
Armageddon. Townsend, G.
Arthur Coningsby. Sterling, J.
Arundel. Cumberland, R.
Athenian Captive. Talfourd, Sir T. N.
Attempts in Verse. Jones, J.
Aurora Leigh. Browning, E. B.

Female Biography. Hays, M.
Female Vagrant. Guilt and Sorrow. Wordsworth, W.
Ferranti and Giulio. Landor, W. S.
Ferryman. Landor, R. E.
Festus. Bailey, P. J.
Fidelity. Wordsworth, W.
Field of Waterloo. Scott, Sir W.
Fifty Years' Recollections. Redding, C.
Fire, Famine, and Slaughter. Coleridge, S.
First Impressions of England. Miller, H.
Flood of Thessaly. Proctor, B. W.
Florence Macarthy. Morgan, Lady.
Foliage. Hunt, J. H. L.
Fool of Quality. Brook, H.
For Each and For All. Martineau, H.
'For honest men of every blood and creed.' Milnes, R. M.
Forest and Game Law Tales. Martineau, H.
Forester. Edgeworth, M.
Forester's Guide and Profitable Planter. Scott, Sir W.
Forge. Whimsicalities. Hood, T.
Fortunes of Nigel. Scott, Sir W.
Foster Mother's Tale. Coleridge, S. T.
Fountain of Arethusa. Landor, R. E.
Four Georges. Thackeray, W. M.
Fra Rupert. Landor, W. S.
Fragment on the Church. Arnold, T.
Frankenstein. Shelley, M. W.
Freiheit. Schelling.
French Wine and Politics. Martineau, H.
Friend, The. Coleridge, S. T.
Friend of Humanity and the Knife Grinder. Canning, G.
Fudges in England. Moore, T.

Gale Middleton. Smith, H.
Gardener's Daughter. Tennyson, A.
Gebir. Landor, W. S.
Geist der Zeit. Arndt, E. M.
General Theorem for A—— College Declamations. Le Grice, C. V.
Geraldine, Agnew, E. C.
German Anti-supernaturalism. Harwood, P.
German Gil Blas. Combe, W.
German Romance. Carlyle, T.
Giaour. Byron, Lord.
Gil Blas. Le Sage.
Gilbert Gurney. Hook, T.
'Giordano, verily thy Pencil's skill.' Wordsworth, W.
Giovanna of Naples. Landor, W. S.
Glencoe. Talfourd, Sir T. N.
'Goethe in Weimar sleeps.' Arnold, M.
Gold-Bug. Poe, E. A.
Golden Treasury. Palgrave, F. T.
Grace Connell. Ireland. Hall, S. C.
Great Expectations. Dickens, C.
Guilt and Sorrow. Wordsworth, W.

III—U

MADE AT THE
TEMPLE PRESS
LETCHWORTH
IN
GREAT BRITAIN